INDIA-BANGLADESH
Fifty Years of Friendship

INDIA-BANGLADESH
Fifty Years of Friendship

Samudra Gupta Kashyap

INDIAN COUNCIL OF WORLD AFFAIRS

PENTAGON PRESS

India-Bangladesh: Fifty Years of Friendship
Samudra Gupta Kashyap

ISBN 978-93-90095-54-4

First Published in 2022

Published by
PENTAGON PRESS
206, Peacock Lane, Shahpur Jat,
New Delhi-110049
Phones: 011-64706243, 26491568
Telefax: 011-26490600
email: rajan@pentagonpress.in
website: www.pentagonpress.in

Printed at Aegean Offset Printers, Greater Noida, U.P.

CONTENTS

1

Bangladesh: A Brief History

Bangladesh was born in March 1971. The land and the people have a much longer history, as old as India, because it was part of India from time immemorial until 1947.

While Stone Age remnants found in Bangladesh are said to be about 20,000 years old, there are strong evidences of early Bengal cities dating back to the Vedic period; the oldest archaeological site at Mahasthangarh in Rajshahi is said to be about 4,000 years old. At least two Bengal kings—Chitrasena and Samudrasena—figure prominently in the *Mahabharata*, while Chandragupta Maurya's kingdom was probably the first central Indian kingdom to have covered Bengal—present-day Bangladesh—too. Portions of present-day Bangladesh were also part of Assam—Kamarupa—at certain points of time in history, with the latter's southern boundary once near the border between Dhaka and Mymensingh districts. The Nidhanpur copperplate inscription, discovered in 1912 in Nidhanpur village in Panchakhanda Pargana of Syhlet district, refers to land grants of Kamarupa king Mahabhutivarman (AD 518-542). There are also references to inhabitants of Kamarupa being called *Sagara-*

anupa-vasin, meaning inhabitants of the marshy land along the seacoast, and *Purva-sagara-vasin*—living on the Eastern Sea, i.e., the Bay of Bengal.

The earliest best-known Bengal king was Sasanka, a contemporary of Harshavardhana of central India, who had united most parts of Bengal after the fall of the Gupta Empire. While Bengal disintegrated after his demise, the dynasties that followed included the Pala, Chandra, Sena, and Deva, until it became a province under the Sultanate of Delhi in AD 1204. The rule of the Pala dynasty (AD 750 to AD 1200) however is said to be the golden age of Bengal's history. The Pala kings patronised Buddhism, and promoted classical Indian philosophy, literature, painting, and sculpture, and it was during this period that Bengali emerged as a strong language.

The Mughals inherited Bengal from the Sultans in the 16th century, but as the Mughal Empire declined, the Nawabs of Bengal took over. In 1757, the British occupied Bengal by defeating Nawab Siraj-ud-Daula in the Battle of Plassey, and set up their first headquarters in Kolkata. Prolonged exposure to British administration contributed immensely to the Bengal Renaissance, which in turn also helped Bengal become a hotbed of India's freedom movement. In 1905, the British split Bengal into two, and clubbed Eastern Bengal and Assam in one province in 1905, with headquarters in Dhaka. Bengal, on the other hand, comprised western Bengal, Bihar, and Odisha. Though Lord Curzon claimed that Bengal was too large to be governed effectively, it was primarily part of a 'divide and rule' policy that effectively segregated the largely Muslim-majority eastern areas from the Hindu-majority western part. Large-scale protests however led to revoking of the partition order in 1911, and the reunification of Bengal. It also saw the separation of Assam, Bihar, and Odisha from Bengal. Moreover, the capital of British India was shifted from Kolkata to Delhi the same year.

When the British left India in August 1947, they also created two nations—India and Pakistan. They practically revived the partition of 1905, and while the larger East Bengal in 1947 went to Pakistan, the smaller part—West Bengal—remained with India. The name 'East Pakistan' however became formally applicable instead of East Bengal only from 1955.

But things did not go well for East Bengal as a part of Pakistan. While Pakistan adopted Urdu and English as official languages, the people of Muslim-majority East Pakistan, who were largely Bengali-speaking, demanded the inclusion of Bengali too. As the movement for recognition of Bengali intensified, the government cracked down on demonstrators in Dhaka on February 21, 1952, killing four students; this day, commemorated as 'Amor Ekushey' (Immortal 21st), has come to be recognized and observed as International Mother Language Day by the UN General Assembly since 2002. Bengali nationalism in East Pakistan reached a peak when the Awami League, established in 1949 by Maulana Bhashani, Shamsul Huq and Sheikh Mujibur Rahman, won a majority in the Pakistani National Assembly election, apart from a huge victory in the Legislative Assembly of East Pakistan in 1970. But instead of letting a new government take charge, a state of Emergency was declared on March 25, 1971, and West Pakistani troops cracked down on Bengali leaders in East Pakistan. The Awami League was banned, its senior leaders taken into custody, and a large number of protestors were killed.

What followed was the Bangladesh Liberation War, particularly after Sheikh Mujibur Rahman delivered a historic speech in Dhaka on March 7, 1971, in which he declared that "*Ebarer songram amader muktir songram, ebarer sangram swadhinatar sangram*" (meaning "the struggle this time is for our freedom, the struggle this time is for our independence"). The crackdown that followed led to one of the worst genocides in human history after the Second World War, in which an estimated three million people were killed. It also triggered off a massive refugee exodus to India, with an estimated 10 million people arriving in West Bengal, Assam, Meghalaya and Tripura between April and December 1971. While the Pakistani Army launched a brutal crackdown on students, the Bengali police and paramilitary forces on March 25, 1971, Sheikh Mujibur Rahman declared the independence of East Pakistan the very next day before being arrested, and asked his people to continue the fight 'till the last Pakistani soldier' had been driven away from Bangladesh.

It was at this crucial juncture that India—the country and its people—stepped forward to extend support to the struggle of the people of East Pakistan. The millions of refugees were provided shelter, food and healthcare. India initially took the stand of not making any direct intervention. As the situation worsened and pressure mounted on the borders, the Indian Army in April 1971 was asked to help the Mukti Bahini. Initially called Mukti Fauj, the Mukti Bahini comprised the East Pakistan Rifles and East Bengal Regiment, and was joined by thousands of young East Bengalis to take on the Pakistani Army and liberate what was named 'Bangladesh'. While the Mukti Bahini fought through nine months, taking on the Pakistani forces, India helped in recruitment, training, and providing equipment to the freedom fighters, besides launching a concerted effort to draw global support for Bangladesh.

Simultaneously, the Indian Army made preparations for war with Pakistan, which began on December 3, 1971, with Pakistan striking first on India. The objectives of the Indian forces were limited—to assist the gallant people of Bangladesh and their Mukti Bahini to liberate their country from a reign of terror and resist aggression on our own land. The war however lasted only 13 days with the surrender of over 90,000 Pakistani troops who were taken prisoners of war.

2

Bangladesh: The Country

Officially called the People's Republic of Bangladesh, the country is surrounded by India on three sides and the Bay of Bengal on the south. It has 4,246 km of international boundary, of which 4,097 km is shared with India and the remainder 193 with Myanmar. Five Indian states share the international boundary with Bangladesh. These are West Bengal (2216.7 km), Assam (263 km), Meghalaya (443 km), Tripura (856 km) and Mizoram (318 km).

The total geographical area of the country is 147,570 sq km, of which 10,090 sq km is covered by water. The country has a coastline of 580 km, and mostly comprises a flat alluvial plain, with a hilly terrain in the south-eastern part covering about 13,295 sq km.

The country is divided into seven administrative divisions—Barisal, Chittagong, Dhaka, Khulna, Rajshahi, Rangpur and Sylhet, which, in turn, comprise 64 districts and 487 sub-districts or *upazillas*.

A riverine country, rivers mark both the physiography of the country as well as the life of the people. Being a gigantic delta formed by the Ganga, Brahmaputra and Meghna, there are about 300 rivers in Bangladesh, 57 of which are trans-boundary ones. Of these, 54 flow from India, and three from Myanmar. These rivers generally flow south. Some of the major rivers are Brahmaputra, Gorai, Jamuna, Karnaphuli, Madhumati, Mahananda, Meghna, Padma, Rupsha, Sitalakhya, Surma, and Teesta. The rivers serve as the main source of water for agriculture, apart from being the principal arteries of commercial transportation. They also provide a large quantity of fish. Floods cause immense hardships during the monsoon, affecting development. However, fresh silt deposits make the soil fertile. The rivers also drain out excess monsoon rainfall into the Bay of Bengal.

What is also very significant about Bangladesh is that it is poised to emerge as a dominant exporter in the years to come. The outbound shipments of Bangladesh have registered an impressive compounded annual growth rate of 8.6 per cent during 2011-2019, compared to 0.9 per cent for India and 0.4 per cent for the world as a whole. This has also led to an increase of Bangladesh's share in world exports from 0.1 per cent in 2011 to 0.3 per cent in 2019. The top five export commodities, including textiles, apparel and footwear, account for more than 90 per cent of the total exports of Bangladesh since 2015, it is said.

While Bangladesh celebrates 50 years of its liberation and the birth centenary of Bangabandhu Sheikh Mujibur Rahman, it recently got the final recommendation to graduate from the status of a Least Developed Country (LDC) to a Developing Country by the relevant UN Committee. Though it will take five more years to actually get that status, it is definitely a reason to rejoice.

SOME INTERESTING ASPECTS OF BANGLADESH

- Eighth largest country in the world in terms of population.
- Constitutionally a secular country with the fourth largest Muslim population in the world and third largest Muslim majority country.Fourth most densely populated country and the most densely populated country in the world having more than 10 million population.
- Situated on the Ganges Delta, the largest in the world, Bangladesh is also the largest wetland in the world.
- Cox's Bazaar is the longest natural sandy sea beach in the world.
- Second largest garments exporter in the world.
- Largest producer of jute (the second largely grown vegetable fibre in the world).
- Sundarbans—common to Bangladesh and India—has the largest mangrove forest in the world.

3

Culture: Language, Literature, Music, Cinema, Sports

Bangladesh has an overwhelming commonness with India in general and with eastern India in particular as far as language, literature, music, folklore, tradition and culture are concerned. Bengali, the language of Bangladesh, is also the principal language in at least two states of India, they being West Bengal and Tripura. While 8.33 crore people in India speak Bengali, about 98 per cent of the 16 crore Bangladeshi people speak one or the other form of Bengali, thus also making Bangladesh the only monolingual country in South-east Asia.

It is important to note that along with the official language of Bengali, the indigenous peoples of Bangladesh speak at least 35 different languages. They include Khasi, Garo, Kokborok, Manipuri, Hajong, Koch, Rajbangshi, Chakma, Santal, Uraon/Oraon, and Munda, which are also spoken in north-eastern India and other parts of eastern and central India.

The Bengalis of India and Bangladesh proudly share the same

history and heritage of the rich language, as was discussed in detail by Dr. Suniti Kumar Chattopadhyaya in his pioneering research work on the Bengali language. Bengalis on both sides of the border also refer to the same lyrical poem—the 8th century *Charyapada*—created by Buddhist monks, as the earliest available literary text in Bengali. Being part of the same country until 1947, the people of Bangladesh today take pride in the contributions of Chandi Das, Daulat Kazi, Alaol, Raja Rammohan Roy, Rabindranath Tagore, Ishwar Chandra Bidyasagar, Michael Madhusudan Dutt, Kazi Nazrul Islam, Sarat Chandra Chattopadhyaya, Bankim Chandra Chattopadhyaya, Mir Mosharraf Hossain, and Kazi Ahdul Wadud, to name only a few in the story of the emergence of modern Bengali literature. Similarly, Bengalis on either side of the international boundary also share common folklore and music. What is most significant is that the national anthems of both the countries were written by Rabindranath Tagore.

Similarly, various forms of folk/tribal music and dance, rooted in the tradition and spirituality prevalent on both sides also share the same roots of indigenous origin. Three most prominent forms of folk songs are *Bhatiali, Bhawaiya,* and *Baul*. Look at the musical instruments—the *banshi* (bamboo flute), the *dhole* (wooden drum), the *ektara* (a single-stringed instrument), the *dotara* (a four-stringed instrument), the *mandira* (a pair of metal bowls used as a rhythm instrument), the *khanjani* and the *sharinda*—belong to the Bengalis in both countries. One cannot also ignore *jatra,* a highly popular folk drama that continues to unite Bengalis in both countries.

When it comes to culinary tradition too, both Bangladesh and eastern and north-eastern India have so much in common. While rice and fish are traditional favourites on both sides, so are sweetmeats from milk products, including the rosogolla. And when one talks about dress, the *sari* and *kurta-pajama* belong equally to the people in both countries.

Among festivals, on the other hand, *Basant Utsab* (spring festival), *Push Mela* (winter fair), *Nobanno Utsab* (new harvest festival), and *Poila Boishakh* (Bengali New Year Day) also unites the people on either side, and so does '*Amar Ekushey*' ("Immortal 21st")—the 21st of February 1952, when five students taking part in a rally to protect the Bengali language were gunned down in the streets of Dhaka—that is observed with due solemnity by Bengalis in both countries.

Though cinema continues to help people of both the countries maintain a close cultural relationship, the screening of commercial Indian films, however, continues to be restricted in Bangladesh since the beginning. Despite that, Indian films, particularly Hindi and Bengali films are highly popular through the Internet. Hardly 100 films are made in Bangladesh every year; but some films do make it to India, especially through the festival route. In January 2021, Bangladesh was the 'Country in Focus' at the 51st International Film Festival of India held in Goa. That Indian filmmakers and artists are deeply revered in Bangladesh can be gauged from the fact that eminent Indian filmmaker Satyajit Ray was the chief guest at the first Shaheed Dibosh of Bangladesh on February 21, 1972 in Dhaka; Shyamal Mitra sang the opening song.

In January 2020, the National Film Development Corporation (NFDC) of India and the Film Development Corporation (BFDC) of Bangladesh signed a Memorandum of Understanding for co-production of a biopic on Sheikh Mujibur Rahman, the founding father of Bangladesh, on the occasion of his birth centenary. The biopic is being directed by eminent Indian filmmaker Shyam Benegal.

Mention must also be made of Bhupen Hazarika, his music, his lyrics and his magical voice, which had cut across political barriers to win a million hearts across both countries. It is important to note that Bhupen Hazarika was the first to have composed and sung a song in Assamese—*"Joijoinabajato Bangladesh, Joijoi Mukti Bahini"*—

aired live by All India Radio, Guwahati, on the morning of December 17, 1971, a day after the Bangladesh War of Liberation ended. Later that evening, he sang the Bengali version of the song from All India Radio, Kolkata.

People in both countries are also bound by the magical voice and music of Bhupen Hazarika, who had won the best music director's award for scoring the music of *'Simana Periye'*, a 1977 Bangladesh film directed by Alamgir Kabir that had won the hearts of millions of people of that country by singing *'O' Ganga boicho keno'* and *'Ganga amaar maa, Padma amaar maa.'* In the latter song, he spoke of the relationship between the two countries thus: *"Ekeia akaash, ekei baataash/ ek hridayeekei to swash"* (meaning "the same sky and same air, same heart and same breath"). What however also stands out is *"Manush manusher jonnye"*, a Bhupen Hazarika song which a Bangladesh poll in 2006 found to be the second most-loved song in that country after its national anthem.

DEMOGRAPHY

Area: 147,570 sq km (10,090 sq km covered by water)

International boundary: 4,246 km (India: 4,053 km; Myanmar: 193 km)

Coastline: 580 km

Rivers: About 300 (57 are trans-border rivers; 54 flow from India, 3 from Myanmar)

Population: 151 million (Census Report of 2011)

Male: 69.51 million

Female: 69.73 million

Sex Ratio: 100.2 (2019)

Population Density/sq km: 1125 (2019)

Infant Mortality Rate (Per Thousand Live Births): 21

Literacy Rate (7+yrs): 74.4% (2019)

Male: 76.5

Female: 72.3

Language:

Bangla (national language) spoken by 95%

English is widely understood and spoken

Religion:

Muslims: 86.6%

Hindus: 12.1%

Buddhists: 0.6%

Christians: 0.4%

Others: 0.3%

Ethnic composition:

Bengalis: 98%

Other indigenous minorities including Chakmas, Marmas, Santals, Garos, Manipuri, Tripura, and Tanchangya: 2%

Source: Bangladesh National Portal

4

India's Role in the Birth of Bangladesh

The Awami League headed by Sheikh Mujibur Rahman had won a majority in the Pakistani National Assembly election of 1970, apart from a huge victory in the Legislative Assembly of East Pakistan. The government in Islamabad however refused to accept it. Instead of letting a new government take charge, a state of emergency was declared on March 25, 1971, and Pakistani troops cracked down on Bengali leaders in East Pakistan. The Awami League was declared unlawful, its senior leaders were arrested, and a large number of protestors were killed.

The situation in East Pakistan turned rapidly from bad to worse with the military crackdown leading to the most inhuman form of genocide, rape, repression and arson by the Pakistani Armed Forces. The crackdown launched by the Pakistani Army on March 25, 1971, to quell what was initially a autonomy movement, but which gradually turned into a freedom movement, by committing atrocities against unarmed Bengalis was codenamed 'Operation Searchlight.'

On 7 March 1971, Sheikh Mujibur Rahman called upon the people of East Pakistan to prepare themselves for an all-out struggle.

The same evening resistance demonstrations began. On March 26, Rahman, before being arrested, declared the independence of Bangladesh and told his people to continue the fight 'till the last Pakistani army' was driven away from the land. One day later, on March 27, 1971, Indira Gandhi, the Prime Minister of India, declared the full support of her government to the Bangladeshi struggle for independence. From March to October 1971, she travelled across the world to mobilize support for the beleaguered people of Bangladesh. Meanwhile, an estimated three million people were killed, thousands of women were raped, and homes destroyed, forcing more than ten million people to leave their land and take shelter in India. That the magnitude of the problem was enormous can be gauged from the fact that the individual population of as many as 84 member-nations out of the then 132 member-nations of the United Nations was less than the number of people who had fled their homes and hearths and taken shelter in India. No other country of the world had faced a problem of such a magnitude at any time of history.

This colossal influx of people from a land that was beginning to emerge as Bangladesh had caused an unprecedented strain on the financial and administrative resources of India. Despite that, however, India decided to provide succour to the refugees on humanitarian grounds. While about 1,200 refugee camps were set up in West Bengal, Assam and Tripura, millions of people also stayed on their own in makeshift camps organised by the citizens of these states. Arrangements were made for the provision and distribution of food, drinking water and medical attention to a population ranging from four to ten million for a period of nine months. Additional resources to the tune of about Rs. 400 crore were mobilised to finance the operations, which also included 'refugee tax', which was collected through various mechanisms including even a surcharge on postal stationery.

India however had from the very beginning made it clear that the Government of India was looking after the refugees on humanitarian grounds, and that it was also the responsibility of the international community to provide relief to them. India had also made it clear that the governments of various countries should use their influence to create conditions in East Pakistan, which would be conducive for the safe return of the refugees to their homeland as early as possible. Responding to this, various UN agencies offered aid to the tune of Rs. 200 crore to the refugees.

Meanwhile, the Provisional Government of the People's Republic of Bangladesh, formed in April 1971, also created a military leadership of the resistance. Initially named *Mukti Fauj*, it drew support from serving military personnel in East Pakistan, while a civilian force was also created alongside. It was a fact that units of the *Mukti Bahini* also trained themselves in the refugee camps inside India, particularly in the three states sharing international boundaries with 'Bangladesh'.

Pakistan, after failing to subjugate the people seeking liberation, turned its war in Bangladesh into a full-fledged one against India, obviously because of the latter's open support to the movement. On December 3, 1971, Pakistan launched a pre-emptive attack on Indian airfields, while a day later the military rulers of Islamabad placed their country in a state of war with India. Left with no choice, India ordered its forces to strike back at the aggressor. The war, which was fought on both the Eastern and Western fronts, lasted 14 days. It culminated in the surrender of over 75,000 Pakistani military and para-military personnel in the Eastern front on December 16. This is considered as one of the biggest surrenders in the military history of the world.

The successful completion of India's military campaign—the 1971 Indo-Pak War, as it has come to be known—for the liberation of Bangladesh within just 14 days and that too across a vast expanse of land criss-crossed by numerous rivers, inhabited by about 7.5 crore people, and held by over 93,000 regular military and para-military troops of West Pakistan origin, has gone down in the annals of military history as a remarkable feat. The Indian Armed Forces adopted a strategy of bypassing the main cities in order to avoid civilian casualties and prevent damage to national assets. The speed of the flanking movement and the determination with which the Indian troops moved ahead, rendered the long-prepared positions of the Pakistani forces untenable.

A landmark event in the rich history of the Indian Armed Forces, this war contributed towards the birth of the independent and sovereign nation of Bangladesh by a campaign finely orchestrated with the *Mukti Bahini*. The military option however was exercised by India only when all political and diplomatic efforts by New Delhi to resolve the issue had failed. The fact however remains that preparation for a war with Pakistan had begun as early as in April 1971.

The Indian Air Force, displayed total mastery of the vast air space, and completely annihilated the Pakistan Air Force within the first 24 hours itself, while the supply and escape routes were completely sealed. The Indian Navy deployed the aircraft-carrier, INS Vikrant, with supporting ships and submarines, which immobilised Pakistani port facilities at Chittagong and in the Khulna-Chulna-Mongla complex. Amphibian landings were carried out at Cox's Bazar to seal off escape routes to Myanmar.

On the Western front, Pakistan's massive offensive thrusts in the Poonch, Chhamb and Rajasthan sectors were effectively blunted, while the Indian Air Force struck without interruption 24x7, targeting aircraft, runways and radar stations. Two daring attacks damaged port and shore installations in Karachi and substantially reduced the strength of the Pakistani fleet.

As the then Indian Prime Minister Indira Gandhi, in her statement in Parliament on December 16, 1971, said, "We hail the people of Bangladesh in their hour of triumph. We hail the brave young men and boys of the *Mukti Bahini* for their valour and dedication. We are also proud of our own Army, Navy, Air Force and Border Security Force, which have so magnificently demonstrated their quality and capacity."

While the War concluded successfully on December 16, 1971, leading to the liberation of Bangladesh, all the Indian forces were withdrawn from Bangladeshi territory by March 12, 1972. Five days later, on March 17, after the total withdrawal of Indian forces, Prime Minister Indira Gandhi visited Dhaka. India has been observing December 16 every year as '*Vijay Diwas*' to mark India's victory over Pakistan in that war.

Apart from honouring the Indian soldiers, the Bangladesh Government, in a special gesture, conferred the Bangladesh Freedom Honour posthumously on Prime Minister Indira Gandhi on July 25, 2011. This was the highest state award given by Bangladesh to any foreigner. Moreover, the Bangladesh Liberation War Honour, 'Bangladesh Muktijuddho Samman', was conferred on former Prime Minister Inder Kumar Gujral and former Defence Minister Babu Jagjivan Ram in 2012, on former President Pranab Mukherjee, former President Fakhruddin Ali Ahmed, former Prime Minister Gulzarilal Nanda in 2013, and former Prime Minister Atal Behari Vajpayee in 2015. A special War Memorial in Dhaka to honour the Indian forces that participated in the 1971 War is proposed.

Indian nationals who received 'Friends of Liberation War Honour' included, among others, included Field Marshal Sam Manekshaw, Lt Gen J. S. Aurora, Lt Gen J. F. R. Jacob, Gen Shankar Roy Choudhury, Air Vice-Marshal Swaroop Krishna Kaul, Maj Gen Lachhman Singh Lehl, Jayaprakash Narayan, former Lok Sabha Speaker Purno A. Sangma, V.K. Krishna Menon, former West Bengal

Chief Ministers Siddhartha Shankar Roy and Jyoti Basu, former Meghalaya Chief Minister Capt Williamson Sangma, Dr. Karan Singh, Nandini Satpathy, Dr. Triguna Sen, Aveek Sarkar, Sardar Swaran Singh, former Tripura Chief Ministers Nripen Chakraborty, Manik Sarkar and Dasarath Deb, P. N. Haksar, Pandit Ravi Shankar, M. F. Hussain, Bhupen Hazarika, Annada Shankar Roy, Raghu Rai, Kaifi Azmi, Salil Choudhury, Manna Dey, Hemanta Kumar Mukhopadhyaya, Ustad Ali Akbar Khan, Amiya Tarafdar, Asghar Ali Engineer, Pritish Nandy, Tarashankar Bandopadhyaya, Nikhil Chakraborty, Sunil Gangopadhyaya, Ritwok Ghatak, Waheeda Rehman, Maitreyi Debi, Rajmata Bibhu Kumari Devi, Rawshan Ara, Begum Sangma, I. P. Gupta, Subrata Roy Choudhury, Bhupen Datta Bhaumik, Bidhu Bhushan Datta, Arundhati Ghose, Zainal Abedin, Dr. Rathin Datta, Sasanka S. Banerjee, Narayan Desai, Dilip Chakraborty, Manosh Ghose, Hiranmay Karlekar, Afzal Hussain, Ahammad Hossain, Biswajit R. Chatterjee, Gouri Ghosh, Shakti Chattapadhaya, K.F. Rustamji, Hiranya Kumar Bhattacharyya, A. B. A. Ghani Khan Choudhury, A. F. Golam Osmani, Jyoti Prasad Saikia, P.C. Sarkar, Debdulal Bandyopadhyaya, Pannalal Dasgupta, Maj Gen S. S. Ubban, Capt Manmohan Sagor Duggal (killed in action), Lance Naik Albert Ekka (killed in action), Asghar Ali, Snehangshu Kanta Acharyya, Angshuman Roy, Somnath Hore, Maulana Syed Asad Madani, Suchitra Mitra, Kulwant Singh Pannu, Kishore Parekh, Subhash Mukhopadhaya, Samar Sen, Subedar Mailkiat Singh (killed in action), Sachindra Lal Singh, Sukhdev Singh Sanhu and Tapishwar Narain Raina. Special 'Friends of Liberation War Honour' awards were also conferred on the 'People of India', the 'Mitra Bahini'—allied forces (meaning Indian forces)—and Akashvani.

Recalling the contribution and sacrifices of the Indian Army, Prime Minister Shri Narendra Modi, during his speech at the 50th National Day programme in Dhaka on March 26, 2021, very rightly stated that soldiers of the Indian Army had fought hand-in-hand with the Bangladeshi freedom fighters, had given their blood and laid down their lives and had played a significant role in the liberation of Bangladesh. He particularly remembered names like Field Marshal Sam Manekshaw, Lt Gen J. S. Aurora, Lt Gen J. F. R. Jacob, Lance Naik Albert Ekka, Group Captain Chandan Singh, and Captain Mohan Narayan Rao Samant among countless others who had taken part in the War leading to the liberation of Bangladesh.

In April 2017, Bangladesh Prime Minister Sheikh Hasina had, for her part, not only honoured 1,661 Indian soldiers posthumously who had fought in Bangladesh's Liberation War in 1971, but had also personally handed over the Bangladesh Liberation War Honour award to the families of 60 Indian soldiers who had died during the liberation war.

The successful conclusion of the war led to the birth of the new Bangladesh nation, and the redemption of India's pledge of sympathy and support to the people of that country. It is also important to recall the kind of support India had extended to Bangladesh immediately after its attainment of Independence. An organised programme for the repatriation of refugees was put into operation from January 1, 1972. Most of the refugees had returned within three months.

India provided the refugees two weeks' ration in kind, journey money, etc., at the time of repatriation, apart from providing transport facilities in most cases. The Government of India also extended financial aid to the Government of Bangladesh to provide each refugee a cash allowance of Rs. 30 per adult and Rs. 15 per child on arrival at their respective destinations in their own country. India also despatched to the new country such materials received from other countries for the refugees in India which had become surplus following their repatriation.

Bangladesh has always remained grateful to India for this

significant role during its liberation war. The relationship between the two countries has been so strong that that it has remained by and large the same despite the change of governments on both sides. Acknowledging India's role in the emergence of Bangladesh, Bangabandhu Sheikh Mujibur Rahman, during his brief stopover in New Delhi on his way to Dhaka after being released by Pakistan on January 10, 1972, had said, "You all have worked so untiringly and sacrificed so gallantly in making this journey possible—this journey from darkness to light, from captivity to freedom, from desolation to hope." His most worthy daughter and present Bangladesh Prime Minister, Sheikh Hasina, had recently said, "We will always remain grateful for the role played by India during our Liberation War. We will never forget it. India gave shelter to more than ten million refugees from Bangladesh." No wonder the bond between the two countries has only grown stronger every passing year.

5

Why India-Bangladesh Relations are so Important

It is a fact often reiterated in Parliament that the Government of India accords the highest priority to relations with neighbouring countries. India is an active political and economic partner of its neighbours and is involved in various projects, including development projects with them. India also has extensive education, culture, trade and investment linkages with neighbouring countries. India's relations with other countries stand on their own footing and are independent of the relations with those countries that are third countries. As far as India-Bangladesh relations are concerned, it is all-encompassing, stretching from closer trade and economic ties to unprecedented security cooperation.

Bangladesh, being one of the most important neighbours of India, relations between them have largely remained warm and friendly, prompting scholars, critics and independent observers to often describe it as a typical textbook example of a neighbourly relationship.

There are a number of issues that remain unresolved between the two countries. They include border, trade, connectivity and transit, water and natural calamities, security including terrorism, defence and strategic matters, and energy, to name a few.

Both Bangladesh and India are members of sub-regional groups including the Bay of Bengal Initiative for Multi-Sectoral Technical and Economic Cooperation (BIMSTEC) and the BBIN (Bangladesh, Bhutan, India and Nepal) initiative, where they look at common ground on issues facing the neighbouring countries. The 'Act East Policy' of India (previously 'Look East Policy') has further reinforced the bilateral relationship. Most significantly, the two neighbours have so far signed more than 100 Memorandums of Understanding (MoU) that cover various sectors including trade, connectivity, and water allocation.

Bangladesh in fact is perceived as a key pillar of India's "Neighbourhood First" policy. The country has benefited from development cooperation worth about $ 9 billion, including $ 7.8 billion in lines of credit at concessional rates. Cooperation between India and Bangladesh has become stronger in areas like tackling emergencies. India had always stood behind Bangladesh during various natural disasters in the past five decades. A recent example has been the cooperation extended to handle the COVD-19 pandemic. While Bangladesh has been the main supporter of India's call for a regional emergency fund to fight the COVID-19 pandemic, New Delhi has also sent, including as grants, vaccine doses in bulk to Bangladesh.

While India was one of the first countries to recognize Bangladesh as a separate and independent state, it was the first to establish diplomatic relations with the new nation in 1971. The relationship between the two countries is based on several commonalities including history, culture and language, and both countries share the same values of secularism, pluralism and democracy. Such has been the relationship that the national anthems of both countries were written by the same person—Rabindranath Tagore. Both countries also subscribe to the principles of sovereignty, equality, trust and understanding, which, in turn, create a win-win partnership that goes far beyond a strategic partnership. This relationship has been only growing stronger each passing year, and has been further reinforced through cooperation in new and high-technology areas.

Thanks to their geographical proximity, India and Bangladesh are also thus bound by a common destiny. With interdependency becoming the key in a globally connected world, this relationship has gained more importance. Cooperation is also crucial in the context of the enormous challenges the two countries face from time to time.

The very first treaty of friendship, cooperation and peace between the two countries signed in Dhaka on March 19, 1972, had focused on maintaining fraternal and good-neighbourly relations and transforming their border into one of eternal peace and friendship; adherence to the basic tenets of non-alignment, peaceful co-existence, mutual cooperation, non-interference in internal affairs and respect for territorial integrity and sovereignty; maintaining regular contacts on major international problems affecting the interests of both countries; strengthening and expanding their mutually advantageous and all-round cooperation in economic, scientific and technical fields, as also in areas of trade, transport and communications; making joint studies and action in fields of flood control, river-basin development, irrigation and hydro-power; promoting relations through art, culture, literature, education, sports and healthcare; not entering into or participating in any military alliance directed against each other; refraining from aggression against each other and not allowing the use of one's territory for committing any act that may cause military damage or threat to the security of the other; and refraining from assisting any third party taking part in an armed conflict against the other party.

Continuing with the tradition set at the time of the birth of the new nation, the two countries had, during the Indian Prime Minister's visit to Bangladesh in May 2012, constituted the India-Bangladesh Joint Consultative Commission (JCC), as envisaged in the Framework Agreement on Cooperation for Development.

That Prime Minister of India Shri Narendra Modi had chosen to visit Bangladesh—his first visit outside the country in the post-COVID period—itself proves how much importance India attaches to Bangladesh. So, in a way, celebration of the golden jubilee of Bangladesh's independence is a kind of joint celebration for both countries. It is a rare case of soldiers of one country laying down their lives for the independence of another country.

As Prime Minister Shri Narendra Modi had, during his speech at the Bangladesh National Day function in Dhaka on March 26, 2021, said that while India has always stood beside Bangladesh through thick and thin, the journey of the two neighbours in the next 25 years of the 21st century is very crucial. According to him, the inheritances of the two countries are common, and so also are their stories of development. Likewise, there is also a commonality between the two nations in their respective goals and challenges, he said, pointing out that while there are tremendous possibilities of sharing the road to development, the challenges posed by terrorism to both countries are also similar. Most importantly, in the words of Shri Narendra Modi, the strength of both the countries lies in the ideals of democracy, and that both countries have a clear vision to forge ahead, come what may. It is of urgent importance to the entire region that India and Bangladesh forge ahead hand in hand.

Bangladesh Prime Minister Sheikh Hasina, on the occasion of the 50th anniversary of her country's independence, had not only acknowledged India's role in the liberation of Bangladesh, but underlined the depth of the relationship between the two countries. "India is not only our next-door neighbour; we have historical, social, cultural ties. The people and Government of India were immensely involved in the evolution process of Bangladesh during our liberation war in 1971, and New Delhi has become one of the best development partners. We share an excellent relationship (with India). I think our mutual ties are at their best now. We want to continue the good relations with our neighbouring nation," she said.

There was a time when the economies of the two countries—and more particularly of Eastern and North-eastern India—were absolutely interdependent. Until 1947, connectivity between the Northeast and the rest of India was through what was then Eastern Bengal. Conversely, Assam and the Northeast were, until India's independence, perfect hinterlands of the economic epicentres of Kolkata and Dhaka. While the Partition of 1947 had cut off vital road, railway and waterway connectivity between the Northeast and mainland India through erstwhile East Bengal, the creation of Bangladesh has only helped restore them over the decades.

Thanks to an increasingly improved relationship, Bangladesh is fast emerging as a connectivity hub not only for India, but also for other neighbours like Nepal, Bhutan and Myanmar. India, for its part, has stepped forward to develop the connectivity network in such a manner that it leads to a perfect sub-regional integration in itself. Bangladesh, in fact, is India's biggest trading partner and destination for India's exports in South Asia. India, on the other hand, is also Bangladesh's second largest source of imports after China.

India's highest number of bilateral treaties is with Bangladesh, and so is the case with Bangladesh. There are over 50 bilateral institutional mechanisms between them, covering numerous areas including security, trade and commerce, power and energy, transport and connectivity, science and technology, defence, rivers, maritime affairs, etc.

It is a fact that the two countries have also faced several common problems and challenges. While tackling natural calamities has been a frequent exercise where both countries have been indulging in holding hands, terrorism is one area in which India and Bangladesh have suffered, and which they have brought to an end through a combined tough stand. With the two countries sharing a porous border, tackling trans-border crimes including terrorism, had called for effective cooperation, which both countries have achieved to a great extent.

That the relationship between the two countries has been becoming stronger by the day was recently reflected when both of them decided to jointly celebrate three events almost simultaneously in 2021—the 50th anniversary of the liberation of Bangladesh, the 50th year of bilateral diplomatic relations between India and Bangladesh, and the birth centenary of Bangabandhu Sheikh Mujibur Rahman. Moreover, participation of a tri-service marching contingent of Bangladesh at the Indian Republic Day Parade in New Delhi on January 26, 2021, further fortified this relationship. Both sides also noted the significance of this event in reminding present generations in both countries about the struggle and sacrifices of the people as well as the forces on both sides leading to the liberation of Bangladesh. Both countries have also decided to commemorate December 6 as "Maitri Diwas", the day on which India formally recognised Bangladesh.

Moreover, the two countries have always maintained very good trade relations. Bangladesh is India's biggest trade partner in South Asia. Trade relations between the two countries is discussed in a separate chapter.

Over the past decade in particular, the economic relationship between India and Bangladesh has entered a new terrain following the strengthening of traditional ties and foundations being laid to deepen and broaden the partnership in going forward. The recent visit of Indian Prime Minister Shri Narendra Modi to Bangladesh to take part in the golden jubilee celebration of Bangladesh's independence and birth centenary of Bangabandhu Sheikh Mujibur Rahman has marked new initiatives to further reinforce the bilateral ties. President Ram Nath Kovind also paid a visit to Bangladesh in December 2021 to participate in the 'Victory Day' celebrations as an honoured chief guest.

In January 2020, the two countries launched a content sharing programme between Bangladesh's state-owned radio public broadcaster, BETAR and All India Radio. The exchange programmes are being broadcast from both India and Bangladesh hourly. The two sides have also agreed to scale up joint production and exchange of programmes between the official broadcasters.

6

Trade and Economic Issues

India was the first country to recognize Bangladesh and both countries have remained committed, from the very beginning, to work in close cooperation. In the very first joint communiqué issued by the two countries at the end of Bangladesh's first Prime Minister, Sheikh Mujibur Rahman's, visit to India on February 8, 1972, it was stated that the two Prime Ministers had, after detailed discussions covering every aspect of mutual relations, expressed their determination to promote, in every possible way, cooperation between the governments and peoples of Bangladesh and India inspired by a vision of lasting peace, amity and good neighbourliness. Since then, there has been a rapid evolution of mutually beneficial economic relations between them, reinforced by regular talks, consultations and visits of delegations, focused on promoting close cooperation in the fields of development and trade.

Economics has always been a significant component in the bilateral relations between India and Bangladesh. Economic relations between them have been multifaceted, and embrace trade transactions, credit arrangements, joint ventures, transit facilities and transport development. Economic relations between Delhi and Dhaka have continued and expanded even during situations when political relations were adverse. This is due to certain objective factors like geographical proximity, commonality of language, matching consumption pattern, similar development needs and experience, and, above all, commonality of the inherited infrastructure.

Trade transactions have played a significant role in strengthening India-Bangladesh relations. While India and Bangladesh had signed their first bilateral treaty on March 19, 1972, economic cooperation between them has accelerated particularly since Bangladesh embarked upon the path of liberalisation in 1982. Both countries have immensely benefitted from the trade relations that grow stronger with every passing year. Thus, while Bangladesh is India's most important export market in the SAARC region today, the same is the case with Bangladesh.

Bilateral trade between India and Bangladesh has grown three-fold over the last decade to USD 10 billion. Bangladesh is today India's biggest trade partner in South Asia; India, on the other hand, is the second biggest trade partner of Bangladesh. The volume of India-Bangladesh bilateral trade was USD 9.5 billion during 2019-20, a slight dip from USD 10.25 billion in 2018-19. While India's exports to Bangladesh during 2019-20 stood at USD 8.20 billion, Bangladesh's exports to India during 2019-20 was USD 1.26 billion.

Both countries are looking to boost Indian investment in Bangladesh and also to augment trade through direct air services, railways, coastal shipping services and inland waterway services. The two countries have also undertaken a joint study on the various aspects of a bilateral Comprehensive Economic Partnership Agreement (CEPA). The terms of reference for the India-Bangladesh CEO Forum, meanwhile, have been finalised, and this is expected to provide policy-level inputs in various areas of trade and investment, apart from facilitating exchanges amongst the business communities on both sides.

Major Indian exports to Bangladesh include rice, sugar, pulses and onions, engineering goods, chemicals and pharmaceuticals, accessories, petroleum products, cotton, sugar, fruits, cereals, vehicles, etc. Bangladesh on the other hand exports a number of items including textiles, plastic goods, cement, furnace oil, batteries, cut flowers, pharmaceutical products, copper wire, melamine, etc.

Bilateral trade in textiles and clothing products between India and Bangladesh is particularly noteworthy in this context. India's major exports of textiles and clothing items to Bangladesh include raw cotton, silk, cotton yarn, denim fabrics, woven and knit fabrics, twill weave cotton, textured yarn, etc. Bangladesh, on the other hand, exports textiles and clothing products to India including jute yarn, men and boys' trousers, sacks and bags, jute and other textile-based fibres, woven jute fabrics, T-shirts and singlets, men/boys' jackets, and blazers, etc.

India and Bangladesh in fact have probably the highest number of bilateral treaties and MoUs among all countries. That the two neighbours lay maximum importance on value bilateral relations is reflected in the increasing number of high-level visits between the two countries every passing year. No wonder the ties between the two neighbours have been described as mutually transformative, and thus potentially benefitting the entire region.

Moreover, India has unilaterally extended duty-free and quota free access to the Indian market to virtually all but 26 Bangladeshi products, as a result of which bilateral trade volumes have increased. India, since 2011, opened its huge markets to Bangladesh under SAFTA, thus allowing exporters from Bangladesh Duty Free and Quota Free (DFQF) market access for 100 percent tariff lines except for alcohol and tobacco. The grant of DFQF market access has played a major part in boosting Bangladesh exports to India, which tripled in a decade and helped reduce, to some extent, the large bilateral trade deficit. In the medium term, this should encourage foreign direct investment into Bangladesh in the manufacturing sector, given that the vast Indian market would also be available to investors.

Traditional river waterways connecting various Bangladesh cities to India that had remained closed since 1965, have meanwhile been reopened. The gradual reopening of these waterways and development of new routes has provided a much-needed fillip to trade and commerce between the two countries. Mention must also be made of the end to the long-pending transit issue. There had been a long-standing request from India for transit facilities through Bangladesh to supply goods to the North-Eastern States, which has been gradually resolved in the past few years. The first breakthrough came in 2010 when Bangladesh approved multi-modal transit of over-dimensional cargo for the Palatana power project in Tripura. The cargo was first transported on barges along the riverine route to Ashuganj and then by road to Tripura. This route was again used later to send steel bars and food grains to Tripura. Subsequently, in 2019, when the Bangladeshi Prime Minister visited India, an agreement was concluded for the use of Chittagong and Mongla ports by India, and in July 2020 a consignment was sent on a trial run to Agartala by using Chittagong. These developments relating to transit and transhipment augur well for the North-Eastern States getting an outlet to the sea through Bangladeshi ports, which was lost in the 1947 partition.

7

Trans-border Issues and Cooperation

India and Bangladesh share 4,096 km of international boundary. Barring a 270-km boundary with Myanmar, close to 95 per cent of Bangladesh's international boundary is with India. Likewise, India too shares its longest international boundary with Bangladesh. Five Indian states share international boundaries with Bangladesh; West Bengal (2,216.7 km), Assam (263 km), Meghalaya (443 km), Tripura (856 km), and Mizoram (318 km).

While the Indo-Bangladesh border is marked by a high degree of porosity, checking illegal cross-border activities and illegal migration have always remained major challenges for both countries. Illegal migration has been a major issue, particularly in Assam, Meghalaya and other north-eastern states of India, and a number of persons who illegally crossed over to India have been handed back to Bangladesh from time to time. There have been regular discussions on trans-border issues between both sides resulting in a series of measures which have paid rich dividends. In order to curb cross-border infiltration, various crimes and other anti-national activities, the Government of India has undertaken the construction of a fence along this border. In 2011, a Coordinated Border Management Plan (CBMP) was signed in 2011 to synergize efforts of the border guarding forces on both sides for more effective control over cross-border illegal activities and crimes as well as to maintain peace and harmony along the India-Bangladesh border.

There have been regular high-level visits and exchanges between the two countries, while frequent visits at the ministerial level as well as between senior officials. On the ground, the Border Security Force (BSF) and Border Guards Bangladesh (BGB) hold meetings at regular intervals to sort out cross-border issues at the local level. It was only in December 2020 that the 51st Director-General Level Talks between the BSF and the BGB were held in Guwahati.

The demarcation of the international boundary at the ground level had remained an issue at certain places for a long time. There were about 170 enclaves in both countries along the border with West Bengal. These enclaves are fragments of a country completely surrounded by another country. While the Land Boundary Agreement between India and Bangladesh was signed way back in 1974, followed by a Protocol in 2011, it was only with the signing of the Land Boundary Agreement in 2015 that these issues were finally amicably resolved.

In May 2015, Parliament passed the historic Constitution (119th Amendment) Bill, thus permitting the exchange of enclaves by India and Bangladesh. Though this mounted to a loss of some territory for India, it however brought to a close the long-standing problem of people living in a stateless situation since 1947. Following this, India and Bangladesh signed the Land Boundary Agreement on June 6, 2015, thus facilitating the transfer of 111 enclaves—covering an area of 17,160.63 acres, from India to Bangladesh. India, on the other hand, received 51 enclaves—an area of 7,110.02 acres—from Bangladesh. Before this, in 2011, India and Bangladesh had signed a Protocol agreeing to maintain the status quo in addressing the issue of adverse possession of land, whereby India would receive 2,777.038 acres from Bangladesh and give away 2,267.682 acres to Bangladesh. However, while the 2011 Protocol could not be implemented due to adverse political circumstances, the 2015 Land Boundary Agreement has brought the curtains down on a whole range of issues arising from the approximately 6.1-km long un-demarcated land boundary in three sectors—Daikhata (West Bengal), Muhuri River-Belonia (Tripura) and Lathitila-Dumabari (Assam); exchange of enclaves; and adverse possessions.

The Land Boundary Agreement came into effect from the midnight of July 31, 2015, with the transfer of 51 erstwhile Bangladeshi enclaves in India and 111 erstwhile Indian enclaves in Bangladesh to their respective countries. Residents of these erstwhile enclaves, who opted to retain their Indian citizenship, shifted to India by November 30, 2015. This was determined based on a joint survey meticulously carried out in the enclaves.

The finest example of cooperation in border management between the two countries however is the Tin Bigha Corridor, an area of about 178 metres × 85 metres, which India had leased out to Bangladesh in 1992 under provisions of an agreement in 1982. The Tin Bigha Corridor, whose land belongs to India, was leased out to Bangladesh at a token annual rent of one Bangladesh Taka per annum (which was however waived by the Government of India), and facilitates a physical link between Dahagram and Angarpota, two villages landlocked in India with Panbari *mouza* of Lalmonirhat district of Bangladesh. People of Dahagram and Angarpota, who had suffered due to non-connectivity since 1947 when East Pakistan was created, finally heaved a sigh of relief.

Both countries have also signed a number of agreements relating to security cooperation. The Coordinated Border Management Plan (CBMP) signed in 2011 has helped synergize efforts of the border guarding forces on both sides to check cross-border illegal activities and crimes as also for maintenance of peace and tranquillity along the border. The maritime boundary between India and Bangladesh, on the other hand, has been settled as per the UNCLOS award of July 7, 2014, thus paving way for the economic development of this part of the subcontinent.

There was a time when people living close to the international boundary on either side had regular economic exchanges. While such activities had closed down in 1971, it was only after the formation of the Awami League government of Sheikh Hasina in Dhaka in 2009 that the *'Border Haat'* (trading market-place for benefit of local people on either side) was conceived And organised on a specific day of the week for a fixed duration where only registered buyers and sellers are allowed to participate. The first Border Haat was opened in June 2011 at Kalairchar (India) between the West Garo Hills district in Meghalaya and Kurigram district in Bangladesh. Since then altogether four Border Haats have been opened in Meghalaya and Tripura, while six more—four in Meghalaya and two in Tripura—are in the pipeline. More haats mean more trade, more people-to-people connects and more trust, one leading to the other.

In March 2021, when Prime Minister Shri Narendra Modi visited Dhaka to take part in the golden jubilee celebrations of Bangladesh's independence, both countries once again resolved to sort out certain pending border issues. These included completion of border fencing in all the pending sectors at the international border between the two countries. Shri Modi and his Bangladesh counterpart, Sheikh Hasina, also agreed to take steps to bring to zero, loss of civilian lives at the border by way of full implementation of the ongoing Coordinated Border Management Plan. Keeping in mind the importance of strengthening the relationship, both leaders laid emphasis on the importance of effective border management to ensure a tranquil, stable and crime-free border.

Equally significant is the settlement of the long-standing maritime boundary dispute between India and Bangladesh, which was carried out as per an arbitration award of the Permanent Court of Arbitration (PCA) under provisions of the UN Convention on the Law of the Sea (UNCLOS). Announced on July 7, 2014, the PCA verdict awarded Bangladesh 19,467 sq km of the 25,602 sq km (74 per cent) of sea area of the Bay of Bengal, leaving 6,135 sq km (24 per cent) to India. While the first Indo-Bangladesh sea boundary discussion was held way back in 1974, Bangladesh approached the PCA at The Hague in October 2009 after a series of bilateral discussions had failed to yield any result acceptable to both sides. The PCA verdict came after nearly five years of arguments and counter-arguments, spot visit by the judges and examination of survey reports. The judgment also gave Bangladesh an exclusive economic zone of 200 nautical miles, the continental shelf beyond the 200-nautical mile economic zone and access to the open sea, which has prevented it from becoming a 'sea-locked country'. The PCA award is significant because both India and Bangladesh have successfully settled their maritime boundary through a legal mechanism under the UNCLOS; this demonstrates that the two neighbours are committed to a peaceful settlement of bilateral issues. Moreover, it is a win-win situation for both of them, because, while Bangladesh has gained on some issues, India has won on some others. While this has opened up prospects for wider exploration for hydrocarbons in the Bay of Bengal, the two neighbours in 2019 signed an MoU for joint cooperation on the Blue Economy, intended at improving human wellbeing and social equity, while significantly reducing environmental risks and ecological scarcities.

8

Military and Strategic Cooperation

India's defence forces—Army, Navy and Air Force—had played a very significant role in the liberation of Bangladesh. Given this backdrop, and given the geo-strategic importance of the Bay of Bengal region, India and Bangladesh have strong defence and strategic cooperation.

There are a number of MoUs in place between Delhi and Dhaka for enhancing cooperation in the field of national security, development, and operational and strategic studies, while an Annual Defence Dialogue (ADD) with Bangladesh was launched in 2018 to strengthen cooperation in this area. Annual staff talks between the Air Force, Navy and Army of the two countries are also being held thrice a year, the Chiefs of Staffs of the three forces exchange visits every year, and joint army and naval exercises have also become an annual affair. Military training and capacity building continues to be a cornerstone of bilateral cooperation.

There are also strong institutional linkages between leading defence training institutions of the two countries in the field of strategic and operational studies, national security, development and strategic studies. While several hundred Indian armed forces personnel attend different training courses in Bangladesh every year, Bangladesh also sends several batches of armed forces personnel for training in India.

These trainings, conducted under Exercise Sampriti in for both countries for Army personnel, are particularly intended at imparting training for counter terrorism; Exercise Milan is meant for Navy personnel. The navies and coast guards of both the countries exchange goodwill ship visits to each other.

Scholarships are given by the Government of India every year to the heirs of *Muktijoddhas* (Bangladesh War Veterans) to pursue higher secondary and undergraduate courses. Moreover, 100 *Muktijoddhas* are provided free medical treatment in various Indian armed forces hospitals every year. Exchange visits of Bangladesh *Muktijoddhas* and Indian war veterans take place in December every year to mark the Victory Day celebrations in Dhaka and Kolkata.

The two countries have also signed MoUs on cooperation for the peaceful uses of outer space, and for nuclear energy. Likewise, there is an arrangement between the Atomic Energy Regulatory Board of India and the Bangladesh Atomic Energy Regulatory Authority for the Exchange of Technical Information and Co-operation in the Regulation of Nuclear Safety and Radiation Protection. Similarly, there is an inter-agency agreement between the Global Centre for Nuclear Energy Partnership, Government of India and the Bangladesh Atomic Energy Commission on cooperation regarding nuclear power plant projects in Bangladesh. The two countries also have an MoU providing for India to extend a line of credit worth US$ 500 million to Bangladesh for the purchase of defence equipment.

That India-Bangladesh strategic cooperation has reached new heights was proved when a 122-member tri-service contingent of the Bangladesh armed forces took part in the Republic Day parade in New Delhi in 2021. Likewise, a 122-member tri-service contingent of the Indian defence forces participated in the Victory Day parade in Dhaka on December 16, 2021. Two Indian naval ships—INS Kulish and INS Sumedha—visited Mongla port in Bangladesh in March 2021.

9

Counter-terrorism Partnership

There is no denying the fact that terrorism remains one of the most significant threats to peace and stability in the region. Given this reality, every time the prime ministers of India and Bangladesh meet, there is a reiteration of their strong commitment to combat terrorism in all its forms and manifestations. There have been occasions when certain international terrorist groups, radical and extremist organisations and some insurgent outfits from India's North-Eastern Region used Bangladesh as a shelter and hideout to carry out anti-India activities.

Such groups had also taken advantage of the porous international boundary between the two countries to sneak into Indian territory, commit various kinds of crimes and illegal activities and then escape to the other side. But, with the political situation in Bangladesh changing over the years, and the bilateral relationship rapidly improving, things have come to near-total control. On January 11, 2010, the two countries signed a significant agreement to combat international terrorism. Guided by the traditional friendly relations between the two countries and their endeavour to contribute to the further development of their bilateral relations, deeply concerned with the expansion of organized crime and international terrorism, and convinced of the need to enhance bilateral cooperation in combating terrorism, transnational organised crime and illicit drug trafficking, this agreement drawn up by the two countries has turned out to be one of the most effective bilateral instruments so far.

Among the highlights of this agreement, intended at jointly fighting terrorism in all its forms, is that India and Bangladesh had decided to (a) exchange information and intelligence on the activities of the terrorist groups and their associates, (b) identify and exchange information on any source of financing of terrorism which may be located in the territory of either country and take steps to seize and confiscate the sources of financing of terrorism, (c) coordinate an approach to combating international terrorism, (d) cooperate and share experience in areas of hijacking, termination, hostage rescue and negotiations and protection of VIPs and innocent victims, (e) facilitate cooperation in preventing access to arms, explosives and other prohibited substances for terrorist activities, (f) enhance cooperation and intelligence sharing between the law enforcement agencies of both countries, and (g) provide mutual assistance including exchange of professional expertise and training of security and law enforcement personnel and organizing seminars and conferences.

Prior to that, India and Bangladesh were also signatories to the BIMSTEC Convention on Cooperation in Combating International Terrorism, Transnational Organised Crime and Illicit Drug Trafficking, which was signed on December 11, 2009. The other countries that were party to this convention were Bhutan, Myanmar, Nepal, Sri Lanka, and Thailand.

It must be put on record that there was a time when insurgent groups from India's North-Eastern Region had not only taken shelter in Bangladesh, but had also set up training camps and used its territory to carry out anti-India activities with the tacit support of certain forces opposed to India and to peace in the subcontinent. The Chittagong arms haul case of 2004 stands out as the most glaring example not only of terrorists using Bangladesh soil for anti-India activities, but also as an instance of their attempt to subvert bilateral relations and disturb peace and stability in the region. Since Sheikh Hasina assumed office in December 2008, things however have drastically changed. In the trial that followed, it was alleged that the consignment was intended for use by an insurgent group from North-Eastern India with the active support of some Bangladeshi officials and forces inimical to India. The present regime in Bangladesh not only dismantled most of the camps (about 100 or so) and hideouts of the militants, but also pushed back their leaders to be arrested in India.

Thanks to the extensive engagements that the Government of India has engaged with the Government of Bangladesh under various bilateral mechanisms, and also thanks to improved relations and increased bilateral cooperation, the Government of Bangladesh has categorically said that it will not allow any anti-India activities on its soil. Having adopted a zero-tolerance policy towards extremist and terrorist elements, and having carried out excellent coordination and cooperation with Indian security and border guarding forces, Bangladesh has, over the years, taken a series of actions against the anti-India activities on its soil. Additionally, Bangladesh's actions on extradition cases and transfer of Indian prisoners under the Transfer of Sentenced Persons (TSP) agreement, including deportation of two top leaders of the proscribed United Liberation Front of Asom (ULFA) to India, have had a tremendously positive impact on the overall situation. Bangladesh has also demolished most camps and hideouts of terror groups and insurgent outfits, forcing their members to flee. This, in turn, has ushered in a new era of peace and development in the north-eastern region in general and Assam in particular.

Besides this, taking up issues related to security, crime, violent extremism, narcotics, fake currency, etc., with the Government of Bangladesh through various bilateral mechanisms have also had a quite a positive impact. This has, in turn, also adversely affected international terror groups backed by another neighbouring country, which were using Bangladesh soil to carry out subversive and anti-India activities.

The prime ministers of India and Bangladesh, on every occasion when they meet, have expressed satisfaction at the extent of cooperation between the two countries on security-related issues. They have also promptly strongly condemned every terror attack in India and Bangladesh and expressed their conviction that the fight against terrorism should not only seek to disrupt and eliminate terrorists, terror organizations and networks, but should also identify, hold accountable and take strong measures against States and entities that encourage, support and finance terrorism, provide sanctuary to terrorists and terror groups, and falsely extol their virtues.

More importantly, the prime ministers of both countries have been unanimous in sharing the view that there should be no glorification of terrorists as martyrs. Additionally, both have often called on the international community to end selective or partial approaches to combating terrorism and, in this regard, jointly called for the early finalization and adoption of a Comprehensive Convention on International Terrorism by the UNGA.

10

Trans-boundary Water Sharing

As mentioned earlier, India and Bangladesh share 54 common rivers, which, in India are called the Ganga, Brahmaputra, Teesta, Barak, and known as the Padma, Jamuna and Meghna in Bangladesh. These rivers directly impact the livelihood of people in the two countries, and thus have always remained one important area of close cooperation between India and Bangladesh.

While the first meeting between India and Bangladesh to discuss the issue of trans-boundary rivers was held in January 1972, the mandate of the Commission that was set up is to maintain liaison between the two countries to maximize benefits from common river systems. The Joint Rivers Commission (JRC) meets almost once every year and has facilitated the signing of a series of water treaties between the two sides. On May 16, 1974, the prime ministers of the two countries signed a joint declaration acknowledging the need for augmentation of the flow in the Ganga in the lean season to meet the requirements of both countries.

Though there were certain difficult issues, as it generally happens, it was in December 1996 that the two countries signed a

30-year treaty on sharing of Ganga water. This has considerably relaxed tensions over the management of the trans-boundary Ganga by way of facilitating sharing of waters during lean seasons, and has been working satisfactorily since.

The two countries have been also working towards a mutually acceptable solution in sharing of the waters of the Teesta and Feni, as also of six other common rivers—Manu, Muhri, Khowai, Gumti, Jaldhaka and Torsa. Both India and Bangladesh have been making an all-out endeavour to conclude the agreements on sharing the waters, particularly of the Teesta and the Feni, that would acceptable to both sides and which protects the interests of all stakeholders.

While most of Bangladesh and several Indian states sharing borders with it are mostly highly flood-prone, the two countries have also put in place a system of transmission of flood forecasting data on major rivers like the Ganga, Brahmaputra, Barak and Teesta during the monsoon season from India to Bangladesh. This has enabled the civil and military authorities in Bangladesh to timely shift the population likely to be affected by floods to safe places.

It was only in March 2021, when Prime Minister Shri Narendra Modi visited Dhaka to participate in the golden jubilee celebrations of Bangladesh's independence, that both sides reiterated their resolve to expand cooperation across an entire gamut of water resource issues including a framework for sharing of river waters, mitigation of pollution, river bank protection, flood management, basin management, etc.

It was during Prime Minister Shri Narendra Modi's visit to Dhaka in March 2021 that Bangladesh Prime Minister Sheikh Hasina reiterated Bangladesh's long-pending request for concluding the interim agreement on the sharing of the waters of the Teesta river. Emphasising that Bangladesh receives its fair share of the Teesta waters, she said it would immensely help alleviate the sufferings and save the livelihoods of millions of people dependent on the

Teesta river basin. The draft agreement on Teesta water was agreed to by both governments in January 2011, and Prime Minister Shri Narendra Modi has made it clear that India was sincerely committed to conclude this agreement in consultation with the relevant stakeholders.

Both countries meanwhile have been waiting for an early finalization of the draft of the interim agreement for sharing of the water of the Feni, which had been agreed upon by them in 2011. It is pertinent to note that both the prime ministers have already directed their respective ministries of water resources to work towards an early conclusion of the Framework of Interim Agreement on sharing of waters of six other common rivers, namely, Manu, Muhuri, Khowai, Gumti, Dharla and Dudhkumar. A, MoU meanwhile is under consideration for utilizing the Kushiara river water for the Upper Surma Kushiyara irrigation project in Bangladesh.

Close on the heels of Prime Minister Shri Modi's visit to Dhaka, senior officials of both sides met in Delhi and agreed to expand cooperation across an entire gamut of water resource issues between the two countries. These included a framework for the sharing of river waters, mitigation of pollution, river bank protection, flood management, basin management, etc. A Joint Technical Working Group will provide inputs on the subject.

Increased cooperation on river basin management will also help the two countries to address larger issues like restoring river navigability, better flood forecasting, and irrigation and drought management; preventing massive land loss along river embankments; reconnecting people along the rivers and strengthening their traditional relationship with rivers; and, above all, harvesting clean renewable energy from these rivers. All these activities are expected to create massive employment and livelihood opportunities and revive lost upstream and downstream industries.

11

Energy, Hydrocarbon and Power Sectors

The very first Treaty of Friendship, Cooperation and Peace signed by India with the new-born People's Republic of Bangladesh on March 19, 1972, in its Article 6 had very specifically mentioned about agreeing to carry out joint studies in certain areas, which included development of hydro-electric power. The Joint Working Group (JWG)/Joint Steering Committee (JSC) on power on the other hand provide an institutional framework to promote bilateral cooperation in cross-border trade of electricity.

Taking off from this, India and Bangladesh have been continuing robust cooperation in the power and energy sectors. There has been significant cooperation between the two countries in the generation, transmission and distribution of electricity, including electricity from renewable or other sources. Cooperation in the power sector in fact has come to be recognised as one of the hallmarks of India-Bangladesh relations. While the two prime ministers had inaugurated the export of power from Tripura to Bangladesh in March 2016, India is currently exporting about 1,200 MW of power to Bangladesh. In fact, the electricity grids of India and Bangladesh have now been linked from West Bengal in the west and Tripura in the east and power is being exported from India to Bangladesh through both transmission lines. Future development of the huge hydro-electric resources in the North-eastern States could lead to the evacuation of this power on a shared basis through Bangladesh. There is also potential for an integrated sub-regional grid linking Nepal and Bhutan through as well as with power trading arrangements in place.

The most outstanding example of India-Bangladesh cooperation in the energy sector is the establishment of the Bangladesh India Friendship Power Company Ltd (BIFPCL), a joint venture between the National Thermal Power Corporation (NTPC) and the Bangladesh Power Development Board (BPDB), which, in turn, is setting up a super thermal power plant in Bangladesh.

While the two governments had signed an MoU in January 2010 to enhance the traditional ties of friendship between the two countries through development of economic cooperation, the NTPC and the BPDB signed an MoU in August 2010 to form a JV company (JVC) through 50:50 equity participation to set up a 2x660 MW coal-based power project in Rampalin Khulna Division of Bangladesh. Following this, the joint venture company, namely, the Bangladesh India Friendship Power Company (Pvt.) Limited—BIFPCL—was incorporated in October 2012, and Power Purchase Agreements (PPA), Implementation Agreements (IA) and Supplementary Joint Venture Agreement (SJVA) signed at Dhaka in the presence of the power secretaries of both countries, the Chairman-cum-Managing Director of the NTPC and the Chairman of the BPDB. The entire power to be generated in the upcoming 1.6 billion US$ Maitree Super Thermal Power Project will go to the Bangladesh Power Development Board (BPDB). The project is scheduled to be commissioned in 2022.

It is worth recalling that during the Bangladesh Prime Minister's visit to India in April 2017, agreements for generation, supply and financing of more than 3,600 MW electricity were signed between Indian public/private companies and Bangladesh. These agreements have provided a major fillip to energy sector cooperation between India and Bangladesh in the last decade.

Meanwhile, India's liberal policy of permitting 100 percent FDI in respect of projects relating to electricity generation, transmission and distribution, is expected to see the participation of Bangladesh in power projects in India, particularly in the North-Eastern states. Such joint ventures in the power sector involving the two countries would facilitate the evacuation of power from North-Eastern India to Bangladesh and through that country to other parts of India.

In December, 2020, India and Bangladesh signed the Framework of Understanding (FoU) on Cooperation in the Hydrocarbon Sector. This is expected to further augment energy linkages between the two countries by streamlining investments, technology transfer, joint studies, training and promoting hydrocarbon connectivity. Additionally, it provides for enhancing cooperation in energy efficiency and clean energy, including in bio-fuels. In line with commitments of both the countries to move towards green, clean, renewable sources of energy, India and Bangladesh have also agreed to strengthen sub-regional cooperation, including with Nepal and Bhutan, apart from strengthening cooperation in the area of power and energy connectivity.

The existing practice of sending diesel from India to Bangladesh is by a 510-km railway route. In September 2018, the prime ministers of the two countries jointly inaugurated the construction of the India Bangladesh Friendship Pipeline (IBFP) Project in order to establish and expand the oil and gas pipeline infrastructure in Bangladesh. The 130.36-km pipeline which will take off from the Siliguri Marketing Terminal (SMT) of the Numaligarh Refinery Ltd (NRL) in India, will transport high-speed diesel to the Parbatipur depot of the Bangladesh Petroleum Corporation (BPC) in Bangladesh. While about 125 km of the pipeline will be inside Bangladesh, the rest of it will be in India. The Rs. 346 crore pipeline project, fully funded by India, will have a capacity to transport one million metric tonnes of diesel per annum.

The ONGC Videsh Ltd., on the other hand, has acquired two shallow water blocks in Bangladesh in consortium with Oil India Limited and is currently exploring them. The possibility of gas grid interconnectivity for the mutual benefit of the two countries is also being explored.

12

Connectivity: Air, Railway, Land and Water Transport

One area that stands out as a good example of friendship and cooperation between India and Bangladesh is connectivity through all modes of transport. The movement of goods by road is operationalised through 36 functional Land Customs Stations (LCSs) and two Integrated Check Posts (ICPs) along the Indo-Bangladesh border. Among them, the Petrapole-Benapole ICP alone handles more than 50 percent of the bilateral trade.

The Protocol on Inland Water Trade and Transit (PIWTT), operational since 1972 and renewed periodically, permits movement of goods over barges/vessels from India through the river systems of Bangladesh along eight specific routes. Through this Protocol, both countries have agreed to make mutually beneficial arrangements for the use of their waterways for commerce between the two countries and for the passage of goods trucks between two places in one country and to third countries through the territory of the other under mutually agreed terms.

As many as eight routes were identified for the purpose, they being (1) Kolkata-Haldia-Raimongal-Chalna-Khulna-Mongla-Kawkhali-Barisal-Hizla-Chandpur-Narayanganj-Aricha-Sirajganj-Bahadurabad-Chilmari-Dhubri-Pandu (Guwahati)-Silghat (Nagaon); (2) Silghat-Pandu-Dhubri-Chilmari-Bahadurabad-Sirajganj-Aricha-Narayanganj-Chandpur-Hizla-Barisal-Kawkhali-Mongla-Khulna-Chalna-Raimongal-Haldia-Kolkata; (3) Kolkata-Haldia-Raimongal-Mongla-Kawkhali-Barisal-Hizla-Chandpur-Narayanganj-Bhairab Bazar-Ashuganj-Ajmiriganj-Markuli-Sherpur-Fenchuganj-Zakiganj-Karimganj; (4) Karimganj-Zakiganj-Fenchuganj-Sherpur-Markuli-Ajmiriganj-Ashuganj-Bhairab Bazar-Narayanganj-Chandpur-Hizla-Bansal-Kawkhali-Mongla-Raimongal-Haldia-Kolkata; (5) Rajshahi-Godagari-Dhulian; (6) Dhulian-Godagari-Rajshahi; (7) Karimganj-Zakiganj-Fenchuganj-Sherpur-Markuli-Ajmiriganj-Ashuganj-BhairabBazar-Narayanganj-Chandpur-Aricha-Sirajganj-Bahadurabad-Chilmari-Dhubri-Pandu-Silghat; and (8) Silghat-Pandu-Dhubri-Chilmari-Bahadurabad-Sirajganj-Aricha-Chandpur-Narayanganj-Bhairab Bazar-Ashuganj-Ajmiriganj-Markuli-Sherpur-Fenchuganj-Zakiganj-Karimganj.

The second addendum to the Protocol on Inland Water Transit and Trade, that was signed in May 2020, has increased the number of river routes between India and Bangladesh to ten. Additionally, it has also connected Tripura to the Indian National Waterways. The trial run on the new route between Sonamura (Tripura) and Daudkandi (Bangladesh) on the Gomti river was successfully conducted in September 2020; this is the first ever export from Bangladesh to Tripura through inland waterways. Another route—Dhulia to Godagiri up to Aricha on the Padma is on the anvil. The second addendum has added five new ports of call and two extended ports of call. Earlier, trans-shipment of goods to the North-Eastern states through Ashuganj river port in Bangladesh, and further through Akhaura-Agartala by road, on the other hand, began in June 2016 under the PIWTT.

In 2017, the Coastal Shipping Agreement was signed, facilitating direct sea movement of containerized/bulk/dry cargo between the two countries. In February 2017, container ship services began between Kolkata and Pangaon (20 km from Dhaka) under this framework. A trial run of trans-shipment of Indian goods from Kolkata to Agartala via Chattogram port was successfully carried out. In July 2020, a trial run was successfully carried for moving goods to and from India through Bangladesh under the Agreement on the use of Chattogram and Mongla Ports.

In July 2020, the maiden container cargo exports from India to Bangladesh using inland waterways reached Pangaon International Container Terminal in Dhaka, thus opening up another opportunity for expanding trade and commerce between the two countries.

Earlier, trains from the North-Eastern Region to Kolkata and other places of mainland India used to pass through East Bengal. However, when Pakistan was created in 1947, the vital railway (and also road) link between Assam/Northeast and the rest of India was abruptly cut off. While a new railway link to Assam was created by the Government of India through the Siliguri Corridor in 1950, seven other railway links, all connecting West Bengal and East Pakistan, however, remained partially operational up to 1965. Though Bangladesh was born in 1971, it was only in the past few years that railway connectivity between India and Bangladesh has been restored for the first time in 50 years.

As on date, five railway routes are in operation between India and Bangladesh. These are Petrapole-Benapole, Gede-Darshana, Singhabad-Rohanpur, Radhikapur-Birol and Haldibari-Chilahati. While these links are from the West Bengal-Bangladesh border, the sixth route, from Agartala (Tripura) to Akhaura (Bangladesh), is expected to be ready by the end of 2021. Work is also underway on the Shahbazpur (Bangladesh)–Mahishashan (Assam) railway link.

While the first link—Petrapole-Benapole—was opened in 2001, the latest, the Haldibari-Chilahati section, was inaugurated by the prime ministers of the two countries through a virtual summit in December 2020. As of now, three express passenger trains run between India and Bangladesh, these being the Dhaka-Kolkata Maitree Express (since 2008), the Kolkata-Khulna Bandhan Express (since 2017) and the Dhaka-New Jalpaiguri Mitali Express (jointly flagged off by Prime Ministers Shri Narendra Modi and Sheikh Hasina on March 21, 2021).

India meanwhile has handed over 10 broad-gauge locomotives to Bangladesh in July 2020. These will help enhance rail connectivity with India and augment Bangladesh's capacity to receive cargo from India and movement of passenger and freight trains within Bangladesh.

Besides passenger trains, the Indian Railways also runs goods train services between the two countries, thus facilitating export-import between India and Bangladesh. While the Container Corporation of India had signed an MoU with the Bangladesh Container Company Ltd. in 2017, a container train service between Kolkata and Dhaka was launched in July 2020. The container train will lead to a five-fold reduction in the cost of import-export between the two countries, reducing the rate from Rs. 7,000 per tonne to Rs. 1,500 per tonne, in comparison to road transport. Additionally, the links will enhance rail network accessibility to the main ports, dry ports, and land borders, which in turn will boost growth in regional trade and encourage economic and social development of the region. The passenger trains, meanwhile, have already increased tourist flows between the two countries, apart from benefitting the trade and tourism sectors in Bhutan and Nepal.

While India and Bangladesh had signed a Trade Agreement in 1980, it was an Agreement on Regulation of Motor Vehicle Passenger Traffic in 1999 that led to the opening of bus services between the two countries. The Kolkata-Dhaka bus service was inaugurated on June 19, 1999, which was followed by the Dhaka-Agartala bus service in 2003. A trial run for a Guwahati-Dhaka bus service through Shillong was made in 2014, but regular service is yet to be launched. A Kolkata-Dhaka-Agartala bus service was also introduced in 2015, followed by a Kolkata-Khulna-Dhaka bus service in 2017.

It is important to recall that India was the first country to start air connectivity with Bangladesh within a few weeks of the liberation of that country. There are currently over 50 flights every week connecting Dhaka with several cities of India. The number of flights between the two countries per week is expected to go up 100 within a couple of years.

A trial run of cargo movement on trucks from Kolkata to Agartala via Dhaka and from Dhaka to New Delhi via Kolkata and Lucknow under the Bangladesh, Bhutan, India and Nepal Motor Vehicle Agreement (BBIN-MVA) was conducted in August 2016. Meanwhile, the two prime ministers in a virtual ceremony in March 2021 inaugurated a vital bridge on the Feni, linking Sabroom in Tripura to Ramgarh in Bangladesh. Chittagong port is only 80 km from this point, and this route is expected to gain immense importance in the future for the North-Eastern states to have a more convenient access to the sea.

India's well-connected rail system was of immense help to supply essential commodities to Bangladesh during the COVID-19 pandemic of 2020, as trade through the land routes were suddenly disrupted. During the lockdown period, more than 800 railway rakes carrying about 1.65 million metric tons of essential items (onions, red chillies, ginger, paddy seeds, etc.) were transported through four existing rail routes between India and Bangladesh.

Bangladesh meanwhile is looking forward to the completion of the 6.15-km Padma Multipurpose Bridge, located 40 km south-west of Dhaka, which will connect Mawa with Janjira, thus linking the south-west of the country to the northern and eastern regions. Expected to be commissioned in mid-2022, it is projected to generate employment opportunities for more than 743,000 people in the region. Apart from drastically improving domestic connectivity in Bangladesh, the bridge will also create connectivity of roads, railways, and energy transportation, which, in turn, will ease international connectivity to India, Bhutan, and Nepal by linking to the Trans-Asian highway (N-8) and Trans-Asian railway.

In this connection, it will be pertinent to note that a new World Bank study has pointed out that transport connectivity between the two neighbours would increase national income by as much as 17 percent in Bangladesh and 8 percent in India. The same World Bank report has also indicated that improved connectivity could yield a 297 percent increase in Bangladesh's exports to India and a 172 percent increase in India's exports to Bangladesh.

13

Healthcare and Tourism

Visa and other formalities for people travelling between the two countries have been revised from time to time. Moreover, there are provisions of short-term double-entry visa, long-term multiple-entry tourist visa, long-term employment visa, medical visa, and a separate visa for students, research scholars, journalists, investors and business-persons, as also a transit visa and emergency service visa—all contributing towards increased travelling by people from both sides. The grant of visas to Bangladesh nationals is governed by the Revised Travel Arrangements signed between India and Bangladesh on 28 January, 2013, and the administrative instructions issued from time to time.

Close to a quarter of the 10 to 11 million foreign tourists arriving in India every year are from Bangladesh. While there are several reasons why such a large chunk of foreign tourists to India are from Bangladesh, three most common reasons are proximity, affordability and cultural affinity. Bangladeshi tourists feel at home when they are in India, having little problems with food, language, accommodation, and climate.

For Bangladesh too, the highest number of in-bound foreign tourists is from India. While proximity, good connectivity and affordability are basic reasons, many Indian Bengalis, whether in West Bengal or other states, have their ancestral roots in Bangladesh and thus have a sentimental reason to visit that country. Hindu tourists generally flock to the 12th century Dhakeswari Temple in Dhaka, while the Jeshoreshwari Temple in Shyamnagar, about 300 km from Dhaka, is said to be one of the 51 *shakti-peeths* where the palms of the Devi are believed to have fallen. Other places which Indian tourists prefer in Bangladesh include the Chittagong Hill Tracts, Sundarbans, Srimangal, Gaur and the Somapuri Mahavihara UNESCO world heritage site.

Earlier, Bangladeshi tourists to India preferred mostly to visit West Bengal. Over time, preferences have begun to change, and Bangladeshi tourists not only visit the Delhi-Agra-Jaipur triangle and make a pilgrimage to Ajmer Sharif, but also head for Assam, Arunachal Pradesh, Meghalaya, Nagaland, Tripura, Manipur, Andaman and Nicobar Islands, Jammu & Kashmir, and South India. At present, the largest Indian visa centre in the world is in Bangladesh, which is equipped to issue, on an average, 5,000 visas every day.

India also gets a sizeable number of medical tourists from Bangladesh. This rising trend of Bangladeshi medical tourists to India has been attributed to the reasonable cost of healthcare in comparison to other countries. Language and food habits also contribute to an increased flow of Bangladeshi medical tourists to India. While the inflow of medical tourists to India from Bangladesh has been going up every year, Bangladeshis constitute about 55 percent of the total medical tourists India gets from other countries.

While India accords the highest priority to Bangladesh under the 'Neighbourhood First Policy', healthcare has emerged as a new significant area of cooperation between the two countries. India has been supporting Bangladesh all through on training, capacity building, and technology transfer in the healthcare sector, including supply of ambulances. In 2019, India extended support for establishment of 36 community clinics in five districts of Bangladesh.

If the COVID pandemic is taken as an example, India has provided three tranches of medical aid to Bangladesh, comprising one lakh hydroxychloroquine tablets, 50,000 sterile surgical latex gloves, 30,000 surgical masks, 15,000 head covers, 50,000 gloves and 30,000 RT-PCR test kits. Six online courses have been conducted, of which one was conducted exclusively in Bengali for Bangladesh, in which 352 Bangladeshi professionals were trained.

India has also sent 2,25,928 lakh doses of COVID-19 vaccines to Bangladesh. Both countries are in active discussions regarding cooperation in the field of COVID-19 vaccine, including Phase-III testing, vaccine distribution, co-production and delivery in Bangladesh. The Government of India also facilitated the repatriation of over 5,500 Bangladeshi nationals from India during the lockdown of 2020.

14

India and Bangladesh in Regional Cooperation

India and Bangladesh play a very significant role in the overall socio-political and economic environment of the region. Apart from their strong bilateral relationship, both countries are members of several regional forums.

Both India and Bangladesh are founding members of the South Asian Association of Regional Cooperation (SAARC). Established in 1985, SAARC is an organization pursuing a common agenda to build a connected and integrated South Asia with the larger aim of promoting the development and progress of all countries in the region. SAARC in fact was established with the signing of the SAARC Charter in Dhaka on December 8, 1985. Besides India and Bangladesh, the other six member-states are Afghanistan, Bhutan, The Maldives, Nepal, Pakistan, and Sri Lanka.

The basic objectives of SAARC are as follows: (a) to promote the welfare of the peoples of South Asia and improve their quality of life; (b) to accelerate economic growth, social progress and cultural development in the region and to provide all individuals the opportunity to live in dignity and to realise their full potential; (c) to promote and strengthen collective self-reliance among the countries of South Asia; (d) to contribute to mutual trust, understanding and appreciation of one another's problems; (e) to promote active collaboration and mutual assistance in the economic, social, cultural, technical and scientific fields; (f) to strengthen cooperation with other developing countries; (g) to strengthen cooperation among themselves in international forums on matters of common interest; and (h) to cooperate with international and regional organisations with similar aims and purposes.

The areas in which India and Bangladesh work hand in hand with the other member-states of SAARC include—Human Resource Development and Tourism; Agriculture and Rural Development; Environment, Natural Disaster and Biotechnology; Economic, Trade and Finance; Social Affairs; Information and Poverty Alleviation; Energy, Transport, Science and Technology; Education, Security and Culture.

The BBIN,—Bangladesh, Bhutan, India, Nepal—on the other hand, is a sub-regional initiative envisioned to improve economic cooperation and connectivity among the four South Asian countries. For India, this initiative allows it to bypass some of the more complex political issues of SAARC and engage in direct discussions on connectivity with Bhutan, Bangladesh and Nepal. This initiative is expected to help landlocked developing countries of the region to integrate more effectively with the global economy. BBIN members had, in June 2015, signed the Motor Vehicles Agreement (MVA), which is designed to enhance economic integration among the four member-countries through effective transit and transport facilitation. The goal is to enhance trade and economic activity, personal mobility, and the effective movement of cargo in the region.

India and Bangladesh are also active members of the Bay of

Bengal Initiative for Multi-Sectoral Technical and Economic Cooperation (BIMSTEC), which was originally formed in 1997 as Bangladesh, India, Myanmar, Sri Lanka and Thailand Economic Cooperation, but got its present name in 2004 after Nepal and Bhutan joined it. The BIMSTEC region is home to around 1.5 billion people who constitute around 22 percent of the global population with a combined gross domestic product (GDP) of a 2.7 trillion economy. Headquartered in Dhaka, BIMSTEC is a sector-driven cooperative organization. It began with six sectors—trade, technology, energy, transport, tourism and fisheries, but later expanded its scope to cover nine more, including agriculture, public health, poverty alleviation, counter-terrorism, environment, culture, people-to-people contacts and climate change.

Bangladesh is part of all three groupings—SAARC, BBIN and BIMSTEC. Additionally, the BIMSTEC secretariat is located in Dhaka. This further reinforces the importance of the India-Bangladesh relationship.

BRICS, on the other hand, is a body formed on the margins of the G8 Outreach Summit in St Petersburg, Russia, in July 2006, and comprises Brazil, Russia, India, China, and South Africa. It brings together the major emerging economies of the world which together comprise 41 percent of the global population. Moreover, they have 24 percent of the world GDP and over 16 percent share in world trade. BRICS countries have been the main engines of global economic growth over the years. Not a BRICS member yet, Bangladesh is soon going to be member of the New Development Bank (NDB), established by BRICS in July 2015. The NDB is an alternative to the USA-dominated World Bank and International Monetary Fund. While Bangladesh had, in 2014 itself, placed a proposal to the NDB to become a founding member, it was only at Indian Prime Minister Shri Narendra Modi's initiative that Bangladesh is heading towards joining the NDB.

15

India, Bangladesh and Climate Change

While South Asia is home to about 1.7 billion people, one-fourth of them continue to live in poverty. Successive reports of the Inter-governmental Panel on Climate Change have predicted a gloomy picture for this region in the years to come.

In recent times, abnormal monsoon patterns and frequent and intense storms have aggravated natural disasters and climate change impacts in the region in general and Bangladesh in particular. Those living in absolute poverty—estimated to be about 600 million—are mostly dependent on climate-sensitive sectors like agriculture, forestry, and traditional fishing for their livelihood and daily needs. Bangladesh has been exceptionally vulnerable to climate change, and cyclones and floods, both caused by climate change, have remained the two most important reasons of large-scale loss of human life in the country every year. Being the closest neighbour that bounds it on three sides, India has always played a crucial and responsible role by being the first responder to any crisis in Bangladesh.

Several studies have forecast different estimates of the likely devastating effects of climate change in the Sunderbans areas in both countries. Global warming, rising sea levels, increased salinity, and river bank erosion could lead to the displacement of millions of people, particularly in Bangladesh. Given this impending scenario, close bilateral cooperation in addressing these issues has become even more urgent.

According to a World Bank report of 2018, over 13 million people in Bangladesh could be displaced by the varied impacts of climate change by 2050, making it the country's biggest cause of internal migration. While Bangladesh comes first on India's priority list in its 'Neighbourhood First' policy, India has also always been the first responder to any crisis precipitated by natural disasters there. Climate change in fact is fast emerging as an important strategic area to further cement a genuine and substantive collaboration between the two countries.

India and Bangladesh have in place an MoU seeking to facilitate cooperation in the areas of conservation of biodiversity, joint management of resources, livelihood generation for poverty alleviation and development, cataloguing of local flora and fauna and studying the impacts of climate change. A working group would be set up to implement action under the MoU. Various other collaborative activities between the two countries also contribute towards jointly tackling different climate change issues.

While climate change has threatened a rise in sea levels, Bangladesh alone is likely to see a 45-cm rise by 2050. This will affect 10-15 per cent land area of the country and directly hit about 35 million people. Moreover, the rise in the sea level will lead to saline water intrusion, thus affecting drinking water supply, agriculture and aquaculture in Bangladesh. The rise in the sea level will also affect India in at least two ways—one, that it will put at it risk in terms of regional growth in cities like Kolkata; and two, it will lead to large-scale migration from Bangladesh.

In 2008, Bangladesh adopted the Bangladesh Climate Change Strategy and Action Plan (BCCSAP), which focuses on six priorities: food security, social protection, and health; comprehensive disaster management; infrastructure development; research and knowledge management; mitigation and low-carbon development; and capacity building and institutional strengthening.

Bangladesh, early in 2021, is also in the process of preparing a Strategic Program for Climate Resilience under the Pilot Program for Climate Resilience of the Climate Investment Fund, which is in line with the BCCSAP. Supported by the ADB, World Bank, and the International Finance Corporation, this would help fortify embankments, raise the coastal greenbelt; improve drainage, connectivity, and water resource management; promote climate resilient agriculture and food security; and ensure that drinking water is safe in vulnerable coastal communities.

In 2011, India and Bangladesh had signed an MoU to set up a working group to study the impacts of climate change, particularly in the Sundarbans, cooperate in the conservation of biodiversity, joint management of resources, livelihood generation for poverty alleviation and development, and cataloguing of local flora and fauna. The MoU was entrusted to the respective ministries of Environment, Forest and Climate Change in the two countries. There is also in place a Protocol on Conservation of the Royal Bengal Tiger of the Sunderbans between the two countries.

Being a signatory of the SAAR Action Plan on Climate Change in 2008, and a party to the SAARC Environment Ministers Dhaka Declaration on Climate Change, Bangladesh also gets much-needed support from India in times of crises.

16

Act East Policy and Bangladesh

Launched in 1991, the Government of India's 'Look East' policy laid extra importance on strengthening diplomatic and economic relations with countries lying to the east of India, particularly the ASEAN and other South-east Asian countries. Renamed as the 'Act East' policy in 2014, it focuses more sharply on the extended neighbourhood in the Asia-Pacific region. The policy, which was originally also conceived as an economic initiative, has gained political, strategic and cultural dimensions including the establishment of institutional mechanisms for dialogue and cooperation. And Bangladesh, being on the top of India's 'Neighbourhood First' policy agenda, is naturally crucial to the 'Act East' policy too.

The Act East Policy also lays emphasis on India-ASEAN cooperation in India's domestic agenda on infrastructure, manufacturing, trade, skills, urban renewal, smart cities, Make in India and other initiatives. Connectivity projects, cooperation in space, S&T and people-to-people exchanges are seen as springboards for regional integration and prosperity.

While Commerce, Culture and Connectivity have been the three main pillars of India's robust engagement with its eastern neighbours through its Act East policy, the focus is on creating multi-modal transport links and facilitating easy cross-border movement of goods and people. Bangladesh has particularly benefitted from this, as has been already mentioned in previous chapters. Bangladesh could link up with sub-regional connectivity projects currently being implemented, such as the Trilateral Highway between Thailand-Myanmar-India and the Kaladan multi-modal transport project between India and Myanmar.

Development assistance in the form of concessional Lines of Credit (LOCs) is extended to various countries by India under the Indian Development and Economic Assistance Scheme (IDEAS) through the Exim Bank of India. Bangladesh is one of the biggest beneficiaries of this assistance, and India has, from 2008-09 to 2020-21, allocated over Rs. 2,000 crore to Bangladesh under its various development partnership programmes. The focus of these allocations has been on Roads, Railways, Power, Shipping, SEZs, Health and Medical Care and Technical Education.

Among the major projects funded and supported by India in Bangladesh are 17 railway projects (nine of which have been completed), eight road projects (of which three have been completed), five port and shipping projects (of which one has been completed), one airport, three power transmission line projects and one telecom project. Transmission lines for power evacuation facilities for the US$ 1 billion worth Bangladesh's first nuclear power plant at Rooppur are also being implemented under the Government of India's Line of Credit extended to Bangladesh. These are expected to act as force multipliers to accelerate regional growth and development, promote people-to-people contacts and encourage trade and commerce between the two countries.

Thanks to the additional impetus provided by the Act East policy, the India-Bangladesh relationship has been broadening day by day. The comfort level has been so high that there is no domain today that is has not been touched, thus making the India-Bangladesh relationship a truly 360-degree partnership.

Digital connectivity being part of the Act East Policy initiatives, Bangladesh has provided vital support to India by providing broadband connectivity of 10 gbps for the North-Eastern Region from Cox's Bazar to Tripura and beyond. This has helped improve the speed and reliability of Internet access in North-east India.

17

North-eastern India and Bangladesh

North-eastern India has a very interesting relationship with what is now called Bangladesh. Way back in 1899, Lord Curzon, on taking over as the Viceroy of India, looked for a way to crush the freedom movement that was beginning to build up across India. In 1905, on identifying Bengal as the hottest breeding ground of freedom fighters, he split the large province into two parts. Eastern Bengal was clubbed with Assam making up one province called 'Eastern Bengal and Assam', with Dhaka as its capital. This was, however, strongly despised by the people of Assam (then comprising almost the entire present-day North-East India barring Manipur and Tripura), as the capital of Shillong had become practically defunct. The partition of Bengal was opposed by the Bengalis too, and as a new movement had picked up against the splitting of Bengal, the 1905 decision was revoked in 1911.

As mentioned earlier, the North-Eastern Region of India had been the worst sufferer due to the partition of the country and creation of East Pakistan in 1947. Such was the situation that vital road and railway communications to the region from the rest of India, which was until then directly across erstwhile East Bengal, was suddenly cut off. It took nearly three years to establish a new railway track and a proper highway to reconnect the North-Eastern Region through the newly-created 22-km Siliguri Corridor. The river route, which however had resumed through East Pakistan after a few years of Independence, was stopped in the wake of the India-Pakistan war of 1965.

The liberation of Bangladesh was thus seen as a major ray of hope as far as the connectivity of the North-East was concerned. After all, the people of the north-eastern states in general and Assam, Meghalaya and Tripura in particular had immensely contributed towards the birth of Bangladesh. Lakhs of refugees from strife-torn East Pakistan were given shelter and all kinds of humanitarian support in the North-eastern states, while groups of young men who constituted the Mukti Bahini even underwent training in secret camps set up in the three North-eastern states which share an international boundary with that country.

North-eastern India, in fact, can be seen as the link between two fundamental pillars of India's foreign policy, they being Neighbourhood First and Act East. Of the 4,096 km of international border between India and Bangladesh, the North-Eastern Region (Assam, Meghalaya, Tripura and Mizoram) together share 1,880 km. Given the age-old ties dating back to the pre-1947 era, the development of the North-Eastern Region is closely intertwined with that of Bangladesh.

While the importance of the North East as India's gateway to East and South-East Asia is being increasingly emphasised, the states of the North-East are also often described as the vital link between two fundamental pillars of India's foreign policy, Neighbourhood First and Act East.

The North-East had remained landlocked since 1947. Such was the scenario that Indian flights between Kolkata and the North-East were not even permitted to fly over East Pakistan space, especially after 1965, forcing them to take a circuitous route through the Siliguri corridor. It was only after the birth of Bangladesh that Indian flights began flying straight across it.

Connectivity being a major hurdle for the region, the increasingly better relationship between India and Bangladesh has benefitted the states of the North East the most. As already mentioned, the river routes between the North East (Assam and Tripura) and Kolkata have been revived after a long time since 1965.

To facilitate NER-Bangladesh border trade in goods and services, the Government of India, through the Office of the Commissioner of Customs in Shillong, has set up 26 Land Customs Stations (LCS) along the NER-Bangladesh borders. The state-wise location of these LCS is as follows: Assam (8), Meghalaya (10), Mizoram (1) and Tripura (7). Most of the trade between Bangladesh and the North-eastern Region flows through Assam, Meghalaya and Tripura, with Meghalaya alone handling about 60 percent of the trade volume.

Exports from North-east India to Bangladesh are distinctly different from major export items from other parts of India to Bangladesh. A look at the product-wise trade between the region and Bangladesh indicates a complementary nature between the resource structure of the North-East and demand structure of Bangladesh. Commodity-wise, the North-eastern Region's exports consist mainly of raw materials like coal, limestone, boulders, petroleum products and agro-horticultural products like tea, ginger and citrus fruits. Imports from Bangladesh to the region on the other hand is mostly finished goods like cement, synthetic fabric, readymade garments, and processed food.

A recent study conducted by the World Bank mentions that transport connectivity between the two neighbours would increase national income by as much as 17 percent in Bangladesh and 8 percent in India. The World Bank is also stated to have indicated that improved connectivity could yield a 297 percent increase in Bangladesh's exports to India and a 172 percent increase in India's exports to Bangladesh. And the North-Eastern Region is waiting to become the biggest beneficiary of this.

With the Protocol on Inland Water Trade and Transit (PIWTT) becoming effective, the first container of goods moved from Kolkata to Agartala using the Chittagong port in Bangladesh. A new inland waterways route connecting Tripura to Bangladesh was also operationalized recently with the first-ever export consignment from Bangladesh reaching Tripura through the waterways. Three particular examples can be immediately cited about improved river-route connectivity between India and Bangladesh which have directly benefited the North-eastern Region. All relate to the movement of huge over-dimensional consignments containing machinery for several industrial projects in the North East–Numaligarh Refinery in Assam, Lower Subansiri Hydro-Electric Project on the Assam-Arunachal Pradesh border, and the Palatana power plant in Tripura.

During 2014 and 2015, when the railway link between Lumding and Badarpur (in Assam) remained suspended due to construction of a new broad-gauge track, landlocked Tripura received its entire supply of rice from Andhra Pradesh through the sea route to Ashuganj river port on the Meghna river in eastern Bangladesh. Thanks to the revised Inland Water Transit and Trade Protocol (IWTTP) having a provision of third-country access with Bangladesh, Tripura also received consignments of petroleum products, apart from food grain through the Ashuganj port. This was nothing but the fruition of a three-year-long diplomatic and strategic endeavour between New Delhi and Dhaka.

The Government of India has plans to set up 20 port townships along the Brahmaputra and Barak river systems in Assam. This will enhance inland water connectivity through Bangladesh and galvanize multimodal linkages in the entire North-East/Bangladesh region.

Meanwhile, even as Prime Ministers Shri Narendra Modi and Sheikh Hasina inaugurated the Maitri Setu on the Feni river connecting Sabroom (Tripura) and Ramgarh (Bangladesh) in March 2021, the capital of Tripura, Agartala, got a direct road link to the international sea port in Chattogram. As Sheikh Hasina said, the opening of any bridge is testimony to Bangladesh's continued commitment to support India in strengthening connectivity in the region.

In December 2020, the Prime Ministers of India and Bangladesh jointly inaugurated the rail link between Haldibari (West Bengal) and Chilahati (Bangladesh). This can help revive the old Siliguri-Sealdah rail route through Bangladesh, once upon a time taken by the Darjeeling Mail. When completed, the pre-1965 rail Kulaura-Shahbazpur link will revive railway connectivity between Karimganj (Assam) and Sylhet (Bangladesh).

The biggest benefit, however, will come from the Agartala-Akhaura railway link, which is expected to be completed in 2020. While the present railway route from Agartala to Kolkata via Badarpur, Lumding, Guwahati, and Siliguri measures 1,590 km, the Agartala-Akhaura link will lead to only a 499-km journey from Agartala to Kolkata through Dhaka. The Agartala-Akhaura rail link will also be part of the ambitious multination Trans-Asian Railway (TAR) project, of which both India and Bangladesh are members. Once the Jiribam-Imphal-Moreh railway line is completed, Kolkata will be directly connected to Moreh on the India-Myanmar border through Dhaka and Agartala. Revival of the pre-1947 railway link between Mahisashan (Assam) and Shahbazpur (Bangladesh) also will provide a big boost to trade and commerce, particularly in Assam's Barak Valley.

The reopening of the Parbatipur-Chilahati railway link meanwhile has enabled Numaligarh Refinery in Assam to export petroleum products directly by railway rakes to Bangladesh. In September 2018 the two countries signed an agreement for a cross-border pipeline to carry one million tonnes of diesel annually from the Siliguri (West Bengal) depot of the Numaligarh Refinery to Parbatipur in Bangladesh. India is investing Rs. 285 crore in construction of this 129-km India-Bangladesh Friendship Pipeline, the foundation of which was laid by Prime Ministers Sheikh Hasina and Shri Narendra Modi in 2018 after signing a Memorandum of Understanding for the project.

Keeping in view the trade potential with Bangladesh, Meghalaya Chief Minister Conrad Sangma in November 2019 made a round road trip from Shillong to Tura through Sylhet and Dhaka. During this trip, he not only interacted with trade bodies of both sides, but also invited students and tourists from Bangladesh to Shillong. A delegation of legislators from Assam visited Dhaka with a similar purpose the same year. In October 2020, India's newly appointed High Commissioner to Bangladesh, Vikram Doraiswami, travelled by road from Agartala to Dhaka to take up his new assignment, documenting every lap of his journey in this process.

Delegations of trade bodies, cultural organisations, Members of Parliament, and other groups of Northeast India and Bangladesh meanwhile have been increasingly visiting each other, while traders and manufacturers have been regularly participating in trade fairs and exhibitions in the North-eastern states.

It was only in March 2021 that the Ministry of External Affairs had organized a North-East Buyer-Seller Meet in Guwahati, to accelerate showcasing products and services of the North-eastern states in various sectors such as Agriculture, Horticulture, Handlooms, Textiles, Handicrafts, Tourism and Hospitality, etc., to neighbouring countries including Bangladesh.

18

Partners in Global Issues

India and Bangladesh have, over the past few years, also emerged as a major partner beyond bilateral cooperation in taking forward regional and global issues. Prime Minister Shri Narendra Modi, during his March 2021 visit to Dhaka, thanked Prime Minister Sheikh Hasina for supporting India in its election to the United Nations Security Council. Both countries agreed to continue working together to achieve early reforms of the UN Security Council, combating climate change, attainment of the Sustainable Development Goals (SDGs) and protection of the rights of migrants. The prime ministers of the two neighbouring countries also affirmed the need for developed countries to fulfil their commitments under the Global Partnership to ensure the means of implementation of the SDGs as enshrined in Agenda 2030.

While India and Bangladesh are important members of several regional organisations like SAARC, BIMSTEC and BBIN, leaders of both countries have also reiterated that given the regional and global economic scenarios following the outbreak of COVID-19, the regional organisations have an important role to play. India being the bigger player in the region, Prime Minister Shri Narendra Modi had recently proposed creation of the SAARC Emergency Response Fund to counter effects of the global pandemic in the South-Asian region.

Bangladesh Prime Minister Sheikh Hasina meanwhile has proposed establishment of a SAARC Medical and Public Health Research Institute in her country, in which India will be required to play a major role. Bangladesh meanwhile has been elected Chairman of the Indian Ocean Rim Association (IORA) for 2021-23, after having served as Vice-Chairman during 2019-21.

IORA is an apex regional organisation of 22 member-states and 10 dialogue partners, stretching from South Africa in the west, running up the eastern coast of Africa, along the Gulf to South and South-East Asia, ending with Australia in the east. It works towards greater maritime safety and security. The objectives of the IORA include promoting sustainable growth and balanced development of the region and member-states; focussing on those areas of economic co-operation that provide maximum opportunities for development, shared interest and mutual benefits; and promoting liberalisation, remove impediments and lower barriers for a freer and enhanced flow of goods, services, investment, and technology within the Indian Ocean rim.

India and Bangladesh support each other's roles in various multilateral fora. India and Bangladesh support each other's roles in various multilateral fora. India supported Bangladesh becoming the current President in the Climate Vulnerable Forum. Likewise, India has also successfully pushed Bangladesh's membership in the New Development Bank. Established by BRICS in July 2015, the NDB is an alternative to the USA-dominated World Bank and International Monetary Fund.

19

India-Bangladesh: People-to-People Relations

Sharing centuries-old bonds of history, culture, language, and other unique commonalities, India and Bangladesh also have a very strong people-to-people relationship. That was exactly why over 1,600 Indian soldiers laid down their lives in a war with Pakistan, the victory in which contributed immensely to the liberation of Bangladesh in the winter of 1971.

Hundreds and thousands of Indian Bengalis have their roots in what is today Bangladesh. While some had migrated to present-day West Bengal in the 18th and 19th centuries, a sizeable section of Bengalis had also shifted in the wake of the Partition of 1947, when East Bengal was made part of Pakistan.

Given this backdrop, for a sizeable section of Indian Bengalis, there exists a sentimental attachment with what is Bangladesh today. In fact, the majority of international tourists to Bangladesh are from India. Many people from West Bengal who visit Bangladesh as tourists had their ancestral houses in what was East Bengal prior to

1971, and thus feel nostalgic while visiting that country. There are Indian Bengalis who also visit Dhaka on February 21, which is observed as Bhasha Dibas or Language Movement Day. It was on this day in 1952 that several students of Dhaka University were killed when Pakistani police forces opened fire on demonstrators demanding recognition of Bengali as an official language of the then undivided Pakistan.

There are also a number of families—both Muslim and Hindu—whose members continue to remain divided between the two countries. Thus, matrimonial relations continue to take place between people of the two countries irrespective of their nationality and religious affiliations.

The national heroes of India, particularly of the pre-1947 era, continue to be revered in Bangladesh too; Rabindra Nath Tagore, Subhash Chandra Bose, Bankim Chandra Chattopadhyaya, are some of them, to name only a few. Likewise, Kazi Nazrul Islam, the national poet of Bangladesh, is equally revered in India. Three Indian filmmakers—Satyajit Ray, Ritwik Ghatak and Mrinal Sen—who are equally respected in Bangladesh, in fact draw their ancestral roots to East Bengal, which is now Bangladesh. The legendary Bhupen Hazarika is equally popular in both countries; "*Manush manusher jonye*", the Bengali version of his original Assamese song "*Manuhe manuhar babe*" was found to be the second most-loved song in Bangladesh in 2006 after its national anthem. And, over and above all, the national anthems of both India and Bangladesh were composed by none other than the first Indian Nobel Laureate, Kaviguru Rabindra Nath Tagore.

Human resource development is a key component of India's development cooperation efforts in Bangladesh through its several ongoing training programs and scholarships. It is also through these programmes that the people-to-people relationship between the two nations is becoming stronger with every passing year. Thousands of students from Bangladesh travel to India every year for higher studies in various subjects. Several hundred Bangladeshi civil servants and judicial officers participate in training programmes in different prestigious Indian academies.

The Indian Council for Cultural Relations (ICCR) awards 200 scholarships every year to students from Bangladesh to pursue under-graduation, post-graduation and MPhil/PhD courses in different educational institutes of India including IITs and NIITs. These students and trainees also act as ambassadors of goodwill between the two countries.

Cultural exchanges form an important component of friendship between the people of the two countries. Special emphasis is laid on promotion of exchanges in the fields of music, theatre, art, painting, books, etc. A bilateral Cultural Exchange Programme (CEP) provides the framework for such exchanges. The Indira Gandhi Cultural Centre (IGCC), established in 2010 in Dhaka, plays an important role in celebrating common cultural links between the two countries. It runs training programmes on Yoga, Kathak, Manipuri dance, Hindi, and Hindustani classical music and organises cultural programmes of renowned artists of India and Bangladesh, which in turn contribute towards promotion of people-to-people contacts. Publishers of both countries regularly participate in book fairs in major cities in either country.

The Indira Gandhi Cultural Centre has organised teaching of Hindi at the Institute of Modern Languages in the University of Dhaka. The ICCR has initiated a Tagore Chair in the University of Dhaka since 2011. The University of Dhaka will soon also have a 'Hindi' Chair under the aegis of the ICCR.

The High Commission of India has been publishing a print and electronic edition of a Bengali literary monthly magazine called 'Bharat Bichitra' for the last five decades. The magazine has a wide readership in Bangladesh.

India and Bangladesh have been organising special programmes to commemorate some eminent personalities of both countries. While the 150th birth anniversary of Rabindranath Tagore and the 90th anniversary of the publication of Kazi Nazrul Islam's famous poem *'Bidrohi'* were jointly celebrated in 2011-12, Bangladesh observed the 150th birth anniversary of Mahatma Gandhi in 2019-20. Bangladesh also issued a special postage stamp in the honour of Mahatma Gandhi in 2020.

In 2021, Bangladesh Prime Minister Sheikh Hasina deeply appreciated the warm gesture of India in organizing various events on the occasion of *'Mujib Borsho'*, the birth centenary year of Bangabandhu Sheikh Mujibur Rahman, the founder of Bangladesh. The two prime ministers in March 2021 also jointly unveiled a commemorative postal stamp issued by the Government of India on the occasion of the birth centenary of Sheikh Mujibur Rahman.

As the 150th birth anniversary year of Mahatma Gandhi and the birth centenary of the Bangabandhu overlapped, a digital exhibition to commemorate the two great leaders of the 20th century was screened in Dhaka. To be also mounted in various cities of Bangladesh and India and in selected cities worldwide, as also at the United Nations, this exhibition is expected to inspire values of justice, equality and non-violence, particularly amongst the youth. Meanwhile, the two countries have also agreed to jointly organize several activities to commemorate two epochal events—the 50th anniversary of the Liberation War and the 50th year of establishment of diplomatic relations between India and Bangladesh—in India, Bangladesh and other countries.

As cinema and music play an important role in bringing about cultural integration between the two countries, cultural troupes and artists from both countries regularly visit each other's countries. Though commercial screening of Indian films—particularly those produced in Bollywood—continues to remain restricted in

Bangladesh, there is a healthy exchange of films between both countries through festivals. Festivals of Indian films in different cities of Bangladesh and of Bangladeshi films in Indian cities have been a regular feature. In January 2021, four Bangladeshi films—"Jibondhuli" by Tanvir Mokammel, "Meghmallar" by Zahidur Rahum Anjan, "Under Construction" by Rubaiyat Hossain and "Sincerely Yours, Dhaka" by Tanvir Ahsan—were showcased in the 'Country in Focus' section of the 51st edition of the International Film Festival of India (IFFI) held in Goa. In February 2021, 32 Bangladeshi films were screened in a Bangladesh Film Festival in Kolkata. Bangladeshi film festivals are also held in other cities of India from time to time, while films from that country also participate in different film festivals across India. Likewise, Indian films too are screened in different festivals in Bangladesh; some of them have also won awards there.

Likewise, sports contingents, from football to cricket, from India visit Bangladesh and vice versa every year, thus contributing towards better relationships between the people of the two countries. Meanwhile, a 100-member youth delegation from Bangladesh has been visiting India every year since 2012 to promote understanding among the youth about each other's countries.

The relationship between India and Bangladesh is so wide ranging and the comfort level on either side is so high that there is no domain today that is left untouched. No wonder it has been also described as a truly 360-degree partnership, one that transcends a strategic partnership, and has been contributing towards the realisation of a dream of a peaceful, prosperous, and progressive South Asia.

20

India's Continuous Support to Bangladesh

India has been extending unstinted support to Bangladesh even before that country was born. As mentioned in preceding chapter, India, both the government and the people, had immensely supported, campaigned for, and participated in the liberation of Bangladesh. A number of Indian defence personnel had laid down their lives in the war with Pakistan that led to the birth of Bangladesh.

Development cooperation between India and Bangladesh thus has emerged as a key pillar of the bilateral relationship. From modest beginnings in the years immediately after Bangladesh was born, India's development cooperation with Bangladesh has grown both in size and coverage. Currently three Lines of Credit worth USD 8 billion are under implementation, making Bangladesh the largest development partner of India. The broad pillars of current development cooperation consist of the following:

The first Line of Credit of US$ 1 billion was extended to Bangladesh in 2010 for developing infrastructure projects, mainly in the fields of railways and public transport. The Government of India had subsequently converted US$ 200 million out of the US$ 1 billion

LoC as grant assistance in June 2012 and increased the corpus to US$ 862 million.

A second LoC of USD 2 billion was announced during Prime Minister Shri Narendra Modi's visit to Bangladesh in June 2015. Under it, 16 projects mainly covering areas of Power, Railways, Roads and Transport, Health and Technical Education, etc., were identified and are currently at different stages of implementation.

The third LoC of US$ 4.5 billion to Bangladesh was announced when Bangladesh Prime Minister Sheikh Hasina visited India in April 2017. Under this, 15 projects covering Power, Railways, Roads and Transport, Health and Technical Education, ITC, Shipping and Solar-based connectivity, etc., were identified and are currently at different stages of approval and implementation.

India also provides grant assistance to Bangladesh for projects under 'Aid to Bangladesh'. A large number of projects such as construction of school and college buildings, laboratories, dispensaries, deep tube wells, community centres, sports stadiums, cultural centres, renovation of historical monuments/buildings, etc., have been financed by the Government of India under this programme. A number of Sustainable Development Projects (SDPs) are also being undertaken under this scheme in different cities of Bangladesh. Moreover, the extended development work of '*Kuthibari*'—the ancestral estate of Rabindra Nath Tagore in Shilaidaha in Kushtia district of Bangladesh—is being carried out with grants from the Government of India.

India is also providing vital assistance to Bangladesh in capacity building and human resource development. Every year, hundreds of Bangladeshi civil servants, judicial officers and police officers undergo training courses in various reputed institutions in India. Similarly, under India's ITEC programme, a large number of fully-paid short term training courses are offered to Bangladeshis in a variety of sectors.

21

Impact on the Neighbourhood

The long-standing friendship and cooperation between India and Bangladesh has caused a lasting ripple effect in other countries of the neighbourhood.

India and Bangladesh are part of several regional initiatives like SAARC (1985), South Asian Preferential Trade Agreement (SAPTA, 1995), and eventually an over-arching regional free trade agreement called South Asian Free Trade Agreement (SAFTA, 2004). The Bay of Bengal Initiative for Multi-Sectoral Technical & Economic Cooperation (BIMSTEC), launched in 1997 and comprising Bangladesh, Bhutan, India, Myanmar, Nepal, Sri Lanka, and Thailand, has identified 14 priority areas mutually beneficial to the member-countries. It aims to accelerate economic growth and social progress among members across multiple sectors—agriculture, climate change, counter-terrorism, culture, energy, environment, people-to-people contacts, poverty alleviation, public health, technology, tourism and fisheries, trade and transport.

Despite these, however, various factors stand in the way of smooth intra-regional economic integration among these countries.

Given this backdrop, four countries of the region formed the Bangladesh, Bhutan, India, Nepal (BBIN) Initiative in 2015, which signed the BBIN Motor Vehicle Agreement (MVA) on 15 June 2015. Developed under the aegis of the South Asia Sub-regional Economic Cooperation programme of the Asian Development Bank (ADB), the basic objective of this Agreement is to ease passenger, personal and cargo movement among the four countries.

The Agreement, among other things, allows vehicles to enter each other's territory by eliminating transhipment of goods from one country's truck to another at the border, thereby eliminating a time-consuming and expensive process. This not only intends to cut down trade costs between nations and facilitate smoother transactions and boost trade, but also to possibly reduce, if not entirely eliminate, some portion of the informal trade going on among these countries.

Designed to also make more efficient the existing cross-border trade and transport in and through the North-Eastern Region of India to and from Bangladesh, Bhutan and Nepal, the MVA, however, is yet to be fully operational. However, things are moving in the right direction for its early implementation.

Meanwhile, the landlocked Himalayan kingdom of Bhutan, since July 2019, has been using Indian waterways to export various goods to Bangladesh. With Dhubri in Assam being the port of call, Bhutan's export consignments have now reduced up to ten days of road travel, and saving about 30 per cent in fuel. Bangladesh happens to be Bhutan's second largest trading partner and is a major importer of items like mandarins, apples, boulders, pebbles and gravel. Separated only by the 22-km wide Siliguri Corridor of India, Bhutan in return gets readymade garments, pharmaceuticals and a sizeable number of tourists from Bangladesh.

Nepal too has begun to enjoy the fruits of India-Bangladesh

cooperation as also because of its participation in the various sub-regional initiatives. While India and Bangladesh had signed a MoU in 1978 to facilitate overland road transit traffic between Bangladesh and Nepal, in 2011, the two countries added new rail routes for facilitating overland transit traffic between Bangladesh and Nepal. While railway connectivity between India and Bangladesh has been restored, the first trainload of fertiliser for export to Nepal was handed over by Bangladesh railways to Indian railways in February 2021.

Meanwhile, Bangladesh has shown keen interest in becoming a partner of the India-Myanmar-Thailand trilateral highway project. While the 13,660-km project is likely to be ready by early 2022, Bangladesh is looking at facilitating better connectivity between Dhaka and South and South-East Asian countries. Once this becomes a reality, India's North-Eastern Region also stands to gain substantially in terms of connectivity.

22

The Future

As India and Bangladesh enter 50 glorious years of friendship and cooperation, Prime Minister Shri Narendra Modi has rightly said that partnership with Bangladesh is an important pillar of India's Neighbourhood First policy. Though there were bad days between the two countries, especially following the assassination of Bangabandhu Sheikh Mujibur Rahman in 1975, Bangladesh Prime Minister Hasina's government has been often rightly credited for restoring the historic ties that Bangladesh had with India.

In fact, being in friendship for half a century, India and Bangladesh have a lot at stake. While both countries are expected to attain steady economic growth in the foreseeable future, there is also much to gain from the well-structured economic and political cooperation that India and Bangladesh have been continuing. That is exactly why Prime Minister Shri Modi had clearly stated during his historic visit to Dhaka in March 2021 to take part in the 50th anniversary of Bangladesh, that India is committed to further deepen and diversify this cooperation.

While India and Bangladesh in March 2021 signed a number of

MoUs covering key sectors such as disaster management, sports and youth affairs, trade, technology and more, Prime Minister Shri Modi has rightly said that these will further strengthen the development partnership and benefit the people of both nations, especially the youth. The Prime Minister's statement carries tremendous significance, because while India has the world's largest young population (over 350 million), Bangladesh occupies the eighth spot with 48 million people in the 10-24 year bracket.

India, Prime Minister Shri Modi said, will continue to support the remarkable development journey of Bangladesh and its people under the dynamic leadership of Prime Minister Sheikh Hasina. Given that the goals of the two countries are the same, joint efforts would make progress faster, he said, adding that it will be for the good of the entire South-Asia that India and Bangladesh move together towards the future. That is exactly why the two governments are making meaningful efforts in this direction.

Bangladesh Prime Minister Sheikh Hasina too has clearly outlined what the relationship between the two countries would look like in the future. "India is not only our next-door neighbour. We have historical, social and cultural ties. The people and the Government of India were immensely involved in the evolution process of Bangladesh," she said on the occasion of 50 years of the birth of Bangladesh. It is important to note that Sheikh Hasina has sincerely acknowledged the all-out support that India had extended to the liberation movement of Bangladesh. Ties between the two countries have escalated to new heights to cover areas of trade, commerce, agriculture, energy and communication, she said.

It is a fact that for quite some time, the relationship between India and Bangladesh was steeped in mistrust, misgivings and suspicion. But then, the political will shown by the top leadership of the two countries has not only contributed towards resolving a number of some long-pending issues, but has also taken the India-

Bangladesh relationship to new heights in the past decade or more, and this, despite the fact that certain issues like cross-border migration and water-sharing remain unresolved.

Bangladesh meanwhile is progressing rapidly on the economic front, and is on the verge of being declared a developing nation. It was on the eve of the country celebrating the golden jubilee of its independence that the United Nations Committee for Development Policy (UN-CDP) had, in February 2021, recommended the upscaling of Bangladesh from the category of Least Developed Country (LDC) to that of a Developing Country. Bangladesh is scheduled to officially become a developing country in 2026.

This is significant for India in that the latter had immensely contributed towards the overall development of Bangladesh since its birth in 1971. It is now for the two good neighbours to build upon the 50-year old friendship and strive to uphold this and jointly explore the possibilities of further strengthening this relationship. As Bhupen Hazarika had once sung—"*Ganga aamaar maa/Paddao aamaar maa/....Epaaropaarkon pare janinaa/ O, ami dui-paare je achi*" (The Ganga and Padma are both my mother/...I do not know the boundaries/Yes, I am present on both sides). Yes, that is the spirit, which has to be carried forward.

Bibliography and References

1. *Glorious Bangladesh*. Ed. Farid Hussain. Pub: High Commission of the People's Republic of Bangladesh, New Delhi, 2020.
2. *Shining Bangladesh*. Ed. Santayan Chakravarty. Pub: High Commission of the People's Republic of Bangladesh, New Delhi 2020.
3. *India: A Reference* Annual. Pub: Publications Division, Ministry of Information & Broadcasting, Government of India, 1973.
4. *The Comprehensive History of Assam*, 5 volumes. Ed. H. K. Barpujari. Pub: Publication Board, Assam. 1990.
5. *The Land of Seven Sisters*. Ed. J. P. Saikia. Pub: Directorate of Information & Public Relations, Government of Assam. 1976.
6. https://pib.gov.in
7. https://www.mea.gov.in
8. https://www.mea.gov.in/bilateral
9. https://unctad.org/topic/least-developed-countries/
10. http://ddnews.gov.in/international/un-body-recommends-bangladesh-graduation-ldc
11. https://www.thedailystar.net/frontpage/news/becoming-developing-nation-bangladesh-reaches-milestone-2052161
12. https://www.orfonline.org
13. https://economictimes.indiatimes.com/news/politics-and-nation/india-is-our-true-friend-bangladesh-pm-hasina/articleshow/79774217.cms?from=mdr
14. https://mofa.gov.bd/site/page/6dde350b-1ca6-4c69-becd-a3f12cf14ac1/Bangladesh—An-Introduction)
15. https://www.mha.gov.in/sites/default/files/AnnualReport_19_20.pdf
16. https://mea.gov.in/lok-sabha.htm
17. documents.htm?dtl/33306/joint+statement+on+indiabangladesh+virtual+summit
18. https://cuts-crc.org/pdf/briefing-paper-role-of-border-haat-in-management-of-india-bangladesh-border.pdf
19. https://cuts-citee.org/pdf/opportunities-for-Inclusive-trade-through-transboundary-waterways-of-the-brahmaputra-river.pdf

20. https://www.thedailystar.net/frontpage/news/prosperous-bangladesh-indias-interest-2045341
21. https://www.hcidhaka.gov.in/
22. https://bangladesh.gov.bd/
23. https://pmo.gov.bd/
24. https://www.saarc-sec.org/
25. https://www.saarc-sec.org/
26. https://www.mha.gov.in/
27. https://www.pmindia.gov.in/en/
28. http://www.bifs.org.bd/home.php
29. https://indianexpress.com/article/opinion/columns/india-bangladesh-relations-narendra-modi-visit-7245361/
30. https://indianexpress.com/article/opinion/editorials/india-bangladesh-relations-narendra-modi-sheikh-hasina-7110534/
31. https://timesofindia.indiatimes.com/blogs/toi-editorials/modi-in-dhaka-india-bangladesh-ties-have-hit-the-right-stride-lets-keep-it-that-way/
32. http://online.assam.gov.in/
33. http://petroleum.nic.in/sites/default/files/vision.pdf
34. https://www.asianconfluence.org

Index

*

Bangabandhu Sheikh Mujibur Rahman at the historic rally at the Race Course Maidan, Dhaka, on March 7, 1971.
(Courtesy: Bangladesh High Commission, New Delhi)

President of India V V Giri visiting a Bangladeshi refugee camp in Jalpaiguri district, West Bengal in November 1971.
(Courtesy: Photo Division/MEA)

Lt Gen A.A.K. Niazi, Commander, Eastern Command of the Pakistan Army (third from right), along with Indian officers (left to right) Vice-Admiral N. Krishnan, Air Marshal H.C. Dewan and Lt Gen Jagjit Singh Aurora proceeding to the surrender ceremony in Dhaka on December 16, 1971.
(Courtesy: Photo Division/MEA)

Refugees along with some Mukti Bahini members, returning to their homes from India after liberation of Bangladesh in 1971.
(Courtesy: Photo Division/MEA)

Bangabandhu Sheikh Mujibur Rahman with Indira Gandhi, Prime Minister of India, during the signing of the Indira-Mujib Treaty on May 16, 1974 in New Delhi.
(Courtesy: Bangladesh High Commission, New Delhi)

Prime Minister of India Manmohan Singh with Sri Lankan President Mahinda Rajapakse, Myanmarese Prime Minister Gen Thein Sain, Bangladesh Chief Adviser Fakhruddin Ahmed, Bhutanese Prime Minister Jigmey Thinley, Nepalese Prime Minister Pushpa Kamal Dahal Prachanda and Thailand Prime Minister Thaksin Shinawatra, at the 2nd BIMSTEC Summit on New Delhi on November 13, 2008.
(Courtesy: Photo Division/MEA)

Prime Minister of India Narendra Modi and Bangladesh Prime Minister Sheikh Hasina meeting at the sidelines of the 18th SAARC Summit in Kathmandu, Nepal on November 26, 2014.
(Courtesy: Photo Division/MEA)

Prime Minister of India Narendra Modi presenting a memento to Bangladesh Prime Minister Sheikh Hasina in Dhaka on June 6, 2015.
(Courtesy: Photo Division/MEA)

Prime Minister Narendra Modi and his Bangladesh counterpart Sheikh Hasina witnessing the exchange of agreements between the two countries in Dhaka on June 6, 2015.
(Courtesy: Photo Division/MEA)

A consignment of 20 metric tonnes of Fully Refined Paraffin Wax produced by Numaligarh Refinery in Assam, being flagged off to Bangladesh from the NRL Marketing Terminal on November 29, 2016 (Courtesy: NRL)

A goodwill rail rake consignment carrying High Speed Diesel produced by Numaligarh Refinery Limited in India proceeding to Parbatipur depot of Bangladesh Petroleum Corporation (BPC) in Bangladesh on April 8, 2017. (Courtesy: NRL)

Contingent of the Bangladesh Armed Forces taking part in the Indian Republic Day parade at Rajpath in New Delhi on January 26, 2021.
(Courtesy: Photo Division/MEA)

Prime Minister Narendra Modi and his Bangladesh counterpart Sheikh Hasina jointly inaugurating a digital exhibition on Mahatma Gandhi and Bangabandhu Sheikh Mujibur Rahman in Dhaka on March 26, 2021. (Courtesy: PIB)

Prime Ministers of India and Bangladesh Narendra Modi and Sheikh Hasina jointly inaugurating various projects in Bangladesh in Dhaka on November 27, 2021. (Courtesy: PIB)

Bangladesh Prime Minister Sheikh Hasina with Prime Minister Narendra Modi and West Bengal Chief Minister Mamata Banerjee during her visit to Shantiniketan on May 25, 2018. (Courtesy: PIB)